MY GOD CAN DELIVER

*A Collection of Poems and Songs
Written by the Late Calverine McLaughlin Hill*

CAROL J. HILL CHATMAN

Copyright © 2021 Carol J. Hill Chatman.

All rights reserved. No part of this book may be used or reproduced by any means, graphic, electronic, or mechanical, including photocopying, recording, taping or by any information storage retrieval system without the written permission of the author except in the case of brief quotations embodied in critical articles and reviews.

WestBow Press books may be ordered through booksellers or by contacting:

WestBow Press
A Division of Thomas Nelson & Zondervan
1663 Liberty Drive
Bloomington, IN 47403
www.westbowpress.com
844-714-3454

Because of the dynamic nature of the Internet, any web addresses or links contained in this book may have changed since publication and may no longer be valid. The views expressed in this work are solely those of the author and do not necessarily reflect the views of the publisher, and the publisher hereby disclaims any responsibility for them.

Any people depicted in stock imagery provided by Getty Images are models, and such images are being used for illustrative purposes only. Certain stock imagery © Getty Images.

Scripture taken from the King James Version of the Bible.

ISBN: 978-1-6642-5075-8 (sc)
ISBN: 978-1-6642-5077-2 (hc)
ISBN: 978-1-6642-5076-5 (e)

Library of Congress Control Number: 2021923743

Print information available on the last page.

WestBow Press rev. date: 12/14/2021

Dedicated with love
to
Marvil and Martha,
Lissa and Ray,
Becky and Ray,
Truman
and
our children and grandchildren
who loved and adored
Mom, Momma, Grandma Hill, Nana

Thank each of you so
much for your
support and encouragement
in helping to make this
publication possible.

Thank you, Karen,
for the lovely photo of Mom's piano
used on the cover of this book.

Thank you, Pam,
for making time in your
very busy schedule
to create the website
on which the video versions
of these songs have been uploaded.

Thank you, Truman,
for putting up with my
hours and hours and hours
of neglecting you
during the
preparation of
this manuscript.
I love you!

PREFACE

Biographical Sketch of
Calverine McLaughlin Hill (1931–2015)

Calverine McLaughlin Hill

Calverine McLaughlin Hill, Singing and Playing the Piano

As the title indicates, this book is a collection of the lyrics/chords of songs written by the late Calverine McLaughlin Hill—affectionately known as Cab, Mom, Momma, Grandma Hill, Nana, Mrs. Hill, and Sis Hill. Calverine was born on March 28, 1931, in a small town called Black Rock, Arkansas, to Calvin and Anna McLaughlin. She was the eldest of her four siblings. During high school, Calverine accepted Jesus as her Savior while attending a revival after the tragic death of a schoolmate.

At the age of seventeen, Calverine married Marvil E. Hill, a riverboat captain who worked on the Mississippi, Illinois, and Arkansas rivers and owned a farm. During the next eleven years, Calverine and Marvil became the parents of three daughters and one son. With her husband's frequent absences because of his employment, the busyness of farm life and raising her family caused Calverine to become lax in attending church services except on Sunday mornings. However, this all changed around 1959, when she wholeheartedly rededicated her life to Jesus and made Him Lord of her life. She began to faithfully take her young family to every church service and actively became involved in a lifetime teaching ministry to children and youth. In later life, she also taught adults.

In the early 1970s, Calverine became inspired to write songs. The lyrics and melodies usually came to her simultaneously. Since she had never had any formal piano lessons, she began teaching herself how to play using chords so that she could include the chords with the lyrics of her songs. In her early years of songwriting, she did not realize the importance of putting dates on her songs, but she began including the dates in the 1980s. Using her beautiful cursive, she carefully handwrote her edited lyrics and chords in spiral notebooks. Two of these notebooks contain the 105 songs found in this book. Concerning her songwriting, Calverine once shared, "Most of the time these songs have been for some reason or another—for something I'm going through or something which someone else is going through—when my heart is burdened for someone."

In 2015, at the age of eighty-four and with her health rapidly declining, Calverine recorded her songs on video for her family so that they, too, would know their melodies. The videos are a priceless treasure for her children, grandchildren, and great-grandchildren. It is their desire that many others will be able to share in this blessing. A website has been created https://www.youtube.com/channel/UCEYrOmshnn0-yge2MDyKFSg so that interested readers can watch Calverine sing ninety-eight of her songs, and two of her daughters sing seven of them. The music and singing are amateur, but the lyrics and melodies are awesome.

NO GOD CAN DELIVER

1.
A
Elijah called Baal's prophets
                      A7
And said, "Build up your altar.
D   A
Put on your sacrifice, and we'll wait and see.
                       D
Then—when—your god doesn't answer,
A   E   A
I'll show you that my God hears and answers me."

Chorus
 A   A7
No god can deliver like my God can deliver.
D   A
No other god can set the captive free.
                   D
No other god can hear me when I pray;
A   E   A
No other god can deliver me.

2.
  A   A7   D
King Hezekiah got notice from Sennacherib saying,
             A
"Oh, King, surrender unto me.

Don't you know it's useless
                        D
For you to try and stop me?
    A   E   A
None of all the other gods could put a stop to me."

(Spoken words): But Hezekiah said:

3.
 A   A7
Daniel in the lion's den; the Hebrew children three,
  D   A
Said, "I tell you, O King, my God can set me free.
                                      D
If He doesn't, I trust Him—for I am in His hand.
 A
Your idol is nothing more
        E   A
Than something made by man."

PUT ON THE ARMOR

Chorus
G
Put on the whole armor of God
          C
That you may be able to stand
              G   D
When the enemy comes against you from every side.
             G
Put on the whole armor of God,
          C
Let's go out and take the land,
      G   D   G
And we'll go forth victorious in the name of God.

1.
  G
Having our loins girt with truth
         C
And the breastplate of righteousness,
        G
And our feet shod
              D
With the gospel of peace.
  G
Taking the shield of faith
      C
To quench the fiery darts,

```
  G                 D
```
We're equipping for battles
```
                      G
```
That we're bound to face.

2.
```
    G
```
Our helmets are salvation,
```
      C
```
Our swords, the Word of God.
```
      G
```
Our orders come in prayer
```
             D
```
Down on our knees.
```
       G
```
Now as a soldier of God,
```
  C
```
We're equipped to fight,
```
        G      D
```
And the ruler of darkness
```
        G
```
Has to flee.

Carol J. Hill Chatman

IT WAS JUST A LITTLE BABY

1.
  A
Have you ever wondered what
          E
The greatest gift could ever be?
                    A
Would it be the largest gift laid beneath the tree?
  D   A
Could it be of diamonds, silver, or gold?
      E   D   A
Or would it be a gift of love, the greatest ever told?

Chorus
A   D   A
It was just a little baby God sent down that day.
  E   A
Sent Him to a manger there upon the hay.
D   A
Every promise God had made all wrapped up in one.
        E   D   A
This was heaven's greatest gift: God's only Son.

2.
  A   E
The shepherds heard the angels say, "Go to Bethlehem."
                                   A
The wise men followed a star that day that led to Him.
     D   A
The light of God shone all around to help to light the way,
    E   D   A
So men could find their way to God every Christmas Day.

Carol J. Hill Chatman

WHATEVER THE COST

1.
```
    A                   E       A
The prisoner stood there, all bound in his sins.
    D         A         E
I listened and heard the judge say,
         A              E          A
"You've broken the law, and now you must die.
       B                    E-E7
So guards, come and take him away."
```

Chorus
```
       A              E       A
Whatever the cost, whatever the cost,
       D         A     E
My debts were too heavy to pay.
       A              E       A
Whatever the cost, whatever the cost,
       D      A    E  A
My Jesus, He paid it that day.
```

2.
```
       A                E       A
All others had fled and left me alone.
       D        A         E
No one would stand by me that day.
```

```
        A                  E         A
Then I heard Jesus's voice so loud and so clear,
            B                     E-E7
That on the cross all my debts He did pay.
```

WHY HEAVEN CARED ENOUGH

1.
  A
Maybe I'm not so very smart,
                                        E
But most things I can figure out and see

The reasoning behind the action there.
                                       A
But one thing I have found still puzzles me.

Chorus
   A
Why heaven cared enough to send its very best
                                E
Is one thing I can't seem to comprehend.

Why heaven cared enough to send its very best.
                                    A
And not just once; He's coming back again.

2.
  A
I've gone to school and have my PhD.
                                E
I've studied math and figured angles, too.

But to try and understand the love of God
        A
Is simply more than I can ever do.

3.
 A
To try to calculate the love of God
         E
Would stagger the computers of our day.

With all the information to feed in,
        A
I'm sure it'd give the answer, "There's no way!"

IT'S WRITTEN DOWN

1.
   G
Perhaps you have heard before about the One whom I adore,
          C   G
How He proved His love for all the world to see.

How He came to earth to die in my place to rectify
       A   D
All the bad things that were wrong with me.
         G
He has proven o'er and o'er, by His sacrifice and more,
        C   G
That I'm fairer than the lilies in His sight.
        C   G
I don't have to worry then, if He'll keep His Word again;
    D   G
I've a contract written down in black and white.

Chorus
 G   C   G
It's written down, the love of God.
          D
The sweetest story ever told
     G
Written there in words so bold.
        C   G
It's written down, the love of God,

How He gave His life for me.
                          C
Written down for all to see.
                   G   D   G
It's written down. It's written down.

2.
G
I feel pampered and secure by this love that will endure.
           C   G
No more worrying that I'll ever walk alone.

He is always by my side to protect me and to guide,
    A   D
And every path I walk's just leading home.
             G
He watches o'er me while I sleep.

There's no need that He can't meet.
               C   G
I feel more protected than a king upon a throne.
         C   G
So don't worry about me 'cause I'm happy as can be.
              D   G
I know the greatest love this world has ever known.

Carol J. Hill Chatman

YOUR PRESENCE

1.
A   E
Let Your presence be in my heart today.
                      A
Let Your presence be in my home today.
                      D
Let Your presence be in the earth and sky
    A   E   A
Till You come back to reign.

2.
 A   E
Without the Spirit of the Lord, we are none of His.
                            A
Without the Spirit of the Lord, we are none of His.
                            D
Without the Spirit of the Lord, we are none of His.
   A   E   A
So fill our cups today.

3.
 A   E
Let Your will be done in my heart today.
                  A
Let Your will be done in my home today.

                           D
Let Your will be done in the earth and sky
       A   E   A
Till You come back to reign.

TAKE THE PIECES, LORD

1.
   C   F   C
Once again, Lord, I'm coming to You
                                  D   G
To ask You a favor, Lord; I don't know what else to do.
   C   F
All around me my dreams tumble down.
             C   G   C
Pick up the pieces, Lord, and turn them around.

Chorus
 F
You can take the pieces, Lord,
    C
That I've torn apart,
    D
And put them back together, Lord,
 G   G7
Close to Your heart.
     C   F
A beautiful pattern I'm sure I'll see
            C   G   C
When I give the pieces, Lord, all to Thee.

2.
```
C                  F         C
```
I had built castles out on the sand,

And when the tide of trials came,
```
 D              G
```
They would not stand.
```
    C                    F
```
So Lord, I'm tracing my way back to Thee.
```
        C              G         C
```
Here's all the pieces, Lord, I give them to You.

I'M GOING HOME

1.
     C   F   C
Beyond this world of sin and pain,
         G   C
I have a home that I can gain.
        F   C
I'll live in peace beyond compare.
       F   G   C
I know by faith I'm going there.

First Chorus
    C   F   C
I'm going home, and it won't be long;
      G   C
I'm going home, where I belong.
         F   C
Won't you share with me those mansions fair?
       F   G   C
There's nothing here that can compare.

2.
     C   F   C
Our friends and loved ones wait inside
        G   C
Those pearly gates, 'cross Jordan's tide.

```
            F             C
How glad and happy we will be
        F    G    C
To be at home eternally.
```

Final Chorus
```
          C             F     C
We're going home, and it won't be long.
              G          C
We're going home, where we belong.
                  F           C
And you can share with me those mansions fair.
              F     G    C
There's nothing here that can compare.
```

JESUS'S TEARS

1.
A   D   A
I've often read the story how Jesus prayed alone
                       E
There in the garden of Gethsemane.
    A
And each time I thought the tears He shed
    D   A
Were for the cross that He would bear,
                   E   A
Not knowing what the greater cross would be.

Chorus
    A
I thought the tears in the garden
      D   A
That became as drops of blood
                      E
Were shed for the cross that He would bear.
    A
But many of those tears He shed
    D   A
Were for His friends nearby,
            E   A
Who soon would flee and leave Him standing there.

2.
   A
When His darkest trials came,
       D   A
No friend stood by His side.
                     E
They all fled away in fear.
   A   D   A
I know that this must have broken the very heart of God
                 E   A
To have Jesus all alone and standing there.

3.
A
Peter said, "I'll go with You, Lord.
   D   A
I'll go the extra mile."
                             E
But Jesus knew that he would soon deny
   A
That he had ever known Him
   D   A
Or had ever been His friend.
                   E   A
It was these things that made our Savior cry.

Carol J. Hill Chatman

GET READY, CHILDREN

1.
 C   F   C
Now Moses thought that he would lead God's army out
                                    D   G
And enter in the Promised Land with a mighty shout.
C   F   C
But when they saw the giants, they began to cry,
                                G   C
"If we trust God's promises, we'll surely die!"

Chorus
 C   F   C
Get ready, children, for that judgment day;
                        D
Get ready, children, we're flying away.
C   F   C
It could be morning, noon, or night.
                    G   C
Get ready, children, to take that flight.

2.
 C   F   C
God said He'd take their children who they said would die;
                                   D   G
He'd take them across Jordan's depths on land so dry.

```
C                            F         C
```
He'd give them the blessings they'd refused that day.
```
                                G     C
```
Don't you know that He can always make a way?

2. (key change)
```
   D                          G     D
```
Now He said to be ready; He'd soon come again,
```
                                E         A
```
And those who are watching can go home with Him.
```
   D                      G    D
```
Will we be like Israel and refuse to go?
```
                             A       D
```
If we do, He'll find someone who won't say no.

Final Chorus
```
   D                      G        D
```
Get ready, children, for that judgment day;
```
                    E
```
Get ready, children, we're flying away.
```
   D              G     D
```
It could be morning, noon, or night.
```
                        A      D
```
Get ready, children, to take that flight.

Carol J. Hill Chatman

THE BLOOD HAS BEEN APPLIED

1.
    D
Loved ones all around me, friends on every side.
      G   D
But even with a crowd around, I was all empty inside.
                                            G
That was before Jesus found me and called me to His side
                       D
And told me I'd not feel lonely
         A   D
Once the blood had been applied.

Chorus
       A   D
Oh, the blood has been applied to my soul.
      A
Oh, the blood has been applied,
   G   A
And I have been made whole.
   D   G
I'm resting in His promises; each day I'm satisfied.
                D
Because of Jesus's love for me,
   A   D
The blood has been applied.

2.
  D
I've shouldered my burdens dutifully each day
      G   D
And tried to stand tall and straight as if I knew my way.
                                  G
But way down deep inside, secretly I cried

Because I had no peace of mind
      A   D
Till the blood had been applied.

TRIED AND TESTED

1.
  G
I've had the devil fight about

Believing in the Holy Ghost.
    C
He tried to keep me out of church
                              G
When others asked, "Who do you love the most?"

But every time I recognized
            C
The devil; he is sly.
                    G
Saying, "Devil, I rebuke you in Jesus's name,"
  D   G
That was my reply.

Chorus
  G
I've been tried, and I've been tested

In so many different ways
      C
That I thought I knew all about
          G
How Jesus works today.

But then another trial came,
                  C
And I was heard to cry,
                                    G
"Oh, Jesus, if you ever send another trial like this,
        D   G
Won't you let it pass me by?"

2.
 G
I've been sick nigh unto death,

And I've been talked about.
 C
They accused me like they did the Lord,
                        G
And it only made me shout.

But then another trial came,
                  C
And I had to ask, "Lord, why?"
                                  G
Then I heard in my heart, "Keep your eye on me.
    D   G
My coming draweth nigh."

3.
 G
I've stood and watched helplessly

Our home burn to the ground.
 C
And not just once—it happened twice,
                           G
And I said, "Lord, You've let me down."

Then I sensed Him calmly speak to me,
                        C
"My child, I'll show you why."
                        G
And when I saw what He showed me,
            D   G
I knew I'd trust Him till I die.

MOTHER'S DAY SONG

(Note: Third verse written by Melissa Hill Dickson.)

1.
C   F C
Every home needs the love of a mother,
 F   C   D   G
Someone to be there to dry tears away.
   C   F C
To wash little hands, to guide little footsteps,
  F   C   G   C
To lead them to Jesus, to show them the way.

Chorus
C   F C
No one can take the place of a mother;
F   C   D G
No one can take her place in a home.
    C   F C
When God thought of love, He created Mother,
   F   C G   C
And made her to be the heart of the home.

2.
 C   F C
Children need an example to follow:
 F   C   D   G
Tenderness, kindness, and selfless love.

Carol J. Hill Chatman

```
   C            F           C
```
Someone there to keep home fires burning,
```
   F      C        G         C
```
To be that example of God's tender love.

3.
```
   C                  F        C
```
Mom, you'll never know how very much
```
   F        C         D     G
```
Your always being there has meant to me.
```
   C                 F       C
```
A shoulder to lean on, a friend I can talk to.
```
   F        C        G    C
```
Thank you for being a friend to me.
```
   F                G       C
```
Thank God for giving my mother to me.

LORD, WE'RE YOUR CHILDREN

1.
D
As God led old Moses
      D7
And Israel out.
   G
He led them toward the Promised Land
           D
With a mighty shout.

He went before them
            G
To keep them safe each day.
        D
And we—just like Israel—
    A   D
Can know He'll make a way.

Chorus
 A
Lord, we're your children,
        G   D
And You've blessed us, this we know.
       A   E   A
As we've wandered in the wilderness of this life below,
     D
You've clothed us, and You've fed us.

                        G
By Your hand we're daily led.
         D   A   D
And by faith we see the Promised Land ahead.

2.
 D
We're pilgrims and we're strangers
                  D7
As we journey on our way.
    G
The world doesn't understand us,
              D
But we're not here to stay.
                                    G
We're headed to a country that they just dream about.
                    D
And just like Moses, we can see
    A   D
Our God will lead us out.

I LOVE YOU

1.
A   E A
Jesus, I just want to tell You that I love You.

                  E
Jesus, I just want to tell You that I know You love me, too.
  A
You had a special place for me on Your family tree,
  D
And no one could fill that place—

No one, that is, but me.
A   E A
Jesus, I just want to tell You that I love You.

2.
A   E A
Jesus, I just want to tell You that I love You.

                  E
Jesus, I just want to tell You that I know You love me, too.
  A
My eyes, my ears, my nose, and both of my hands
  D
Are very important parts of Your master plan.
A   E A
Jesus, I just want to tell You that I love You.

Carol J. Hill Chatman

3.
A   E   A
Jesus, I just want to tell You that I love You.
                                                E
Jesus, I just want to tell You that I know You love me, too.
     A
My smile, my height, my hair, my personality
      D
Were all compiled by You, Lord,

Especially for me.
A   E   A
Jesus, I just want to tell You that I love You.
A   E   A
Jesus, I just want to tell You that I love You.

DECISIONS THAT WE MAKE

1.
  A   D   A
One day I took my Bible and proceeded to read
                                              E
How there was a garden that provided every need,
  A   D   A
How Adam and Eve could live in a paradise each day.
D   A   E   A
But because of choices, they threw it all away.

Chorus
D   A
Every day's a building stone we hold in our hand,
                              B   E
And decisions that we make can make or ruin our plans.
A   D   A
By the choices that we make, we plan what we will be;
     D   A   E   A
And with each stone we put in place, we build our destiny.

2.
  A   D   A
I read how God led Abraham to a land he could not see
                                        E
And told him that his children could have that land for free.

```
    A              D              A
And farther on I saw Abraham ventured out
   D              A              E              A
To take God at His Word; changed his life, there is no doubt.
```

3.
```
    A                  D              A
Then I saw old Moses standing by the sea.
                                                    E
I said, "God, if they believed, I'm sure there's hope for me.
    A                      D              A
I know that those same promises await for me today,
   D              A              E              A
And nothing that the devil does can take my faith away."
```

4.
```
    A              D              A
There, Enoch and Noah, Isaac and Jacob too—
                                            E
All in a place of honor—there's nothing He can't do.
    A                  D              A
So with the Hebrew children I would like to say,
   D        A      E              A
"My God can deliver; He's still God today."
```

WHO WILL ROLL THE STONE AWAY?

1.
```
C                           F              C
```
Mary said, "Mister, can you tell me where He lies?
```
                        G
```
Someone has taken Him away."
```
C                           F              C
```
Only when He spoke her name did she understand
```
                    G           C
```
That it was Jesus who spoke with her that day.

Chorus
```
   C
```
"Who will roll the stone away?
```
   F        C
```
Who will let us in?"
```
                              G
```
You could hear the women on their way.
```
   C
```
"Who will roll the stone away?
```
       F        C
```
How can we get to Him?
```
                G       C
```
Why, oh why was He taken away?"

Carol J. Hill Chatman

2.
```
C                      F         C
```
Jesus helped Mary to understand
```
                                    G
```
That it was He there, standing by her side.
```
        C                 F                    C
```
He asked her to tell the others He was very much alive.
```
                  G           C
```
It was for them that He had lived and died.

3.
```
        C                           F        C
```
"The angel rolled the stone away; the angel let us in,"
```
                                  G
```
You could hear the women on their way.
```
        C                         F           C
```
The angel rolled the stone away, now we can get to Him.
```
                         G          C
```
He conquered death and hell that Easter Day.

I WILL NEVER WALK ALONE

1.
   A   D
I played the part of a fool; I walked with the crowd,
   E   A
Though I knew the path they chose was wrong.
                        D
Finally, so ashamed, I realized I was lost.
    E   A
That's when I turned around and started home.

Chorus
A   D
I will never walk alone for He is by my side,
    E   A
No matter what my problem may be.
              A7   D
Tho others may forsake when I need someone close by;
E   A
He will never turn away from me.

2.
   A   D
Like the prodigal son, I may wander far from home,
   E   A
Demanding the biggest share for me.

Carol J. Hill Chatman

                            D
But my Father is waiting to welcome me back
      E   A
After this old world has made a fool of me.

3.
    A   D
He saw me coming home; He killed the fatted calf—
E   A
Just a servant let me be.
                                         D
But no, He's holding out the robe and ring of sonship, too,
      E   A
And reaching out His arms to welcome me.

I'VE READ IN MY BIBLE

1.
     C   C7
I've read in my Bible of a beautiful country
        F   C
Where no one ever will die,

And how that the King who rules on the throne there
      D   G
Will dry every tear from my eye.
     C   C7
I've read that the rivers run ever pure water,
       F   C
And the streets there are made of pure gold.
     F   C
And the leaves of its trees will be for our healing,
           G   C
And we'll live there while ages shall roll.

2.
    C   C7
I've read there's a river that one day I'll be crossing,
     F   C
Like Israel did long, long ago.

And as I step in the waves they will roll back,
     D   G
And on dry ground I'll cross to that shore.

Carol J. Hill Chatman

```
      C
I've read there's a mansion prepared and all waiting,
      F                C
And my Lord, His face I'll see.
         F                    C
In that beautiful somewhere, where loved ones are waiting,
                        G        C
No more heartaches are waiting for me.


3. (key change)
         D                          D7
I've read that no tears will ere mar its beauty,
         G                  D
And no locks need be placed on a door.

There'll never be hatred or cursing or cross words
         E           A
That we'll ever hear anymore.
         D
I've read that its people, all will be holy.
         G           D
No sin in that city we'll see
         G           D
For God in His glory will rule there forever.
              A        D
This will be heaven to me.
```

FIRE ON THE ALTAR

1.
  A   D   A
Someone is sick, someone's loved one astray,
                      E
Another a bill they cannot pay.
  A   D   A
A problem, a heartache, or maybe just grief—
                   E   A
All of our answers are found on our knees.

Chorus
  A   D   A
With fire on the altar and saints on their knees,
          B   E
Praying to God to hear their pleas.
      A   D   A
Well, the devil's defeated and has to leave,
                E   A
With fire on the altar and saints on their knees.

2.
A   D   A
So much corruption and sin about,
                     E
Divisions within and fightings without.

Carol J. Hill Chatman

```
    A                   D        A
No love for the neighbor as onward we trod,
                           E          A
We're fighting a battle we should give to God.
```

3.
```
    A                   D         A
The family's divided, each going their way.
                              E
The children are crying and hurting today.
    A                   D         A
What is the answer? Can you tell me, please?
                           E          A
It's fire on the altar and saints on their knees.
```

WE ARE PREDESTINED

1.
    D
Before I was born, God had a plan
  G
That He'd lead me safely to that Promised Land.
D
And like our father Abraham,
      E   A
I'm walking now by faith as He holds my hand.
         D
He's not willing any perish, so you, too,
G
Can come along, and He'll walk with you.
  D
Don't let the devil stop you; it's just ahead,
          A   D
This place that God has said.

Chorus
   D
We're predestined to a kingdom
    G   D
Prepared by God's own Son.

We're predestined to a kingdom,
    E   A
Each and every one.

Carol J. Hill Chatman

   D
The Father, the Son, and the Holy Ghost
G
Will be our most gracious host.
D
We're predestined to a kingdom,
         A   D
Prepared by God's own Son.

2.
  D
We're the only ones who can mess up God's plan.
G
He's already bought our ticket to that Holy Land.
D
He gave it to us, and He showed us the way
     E   A
And said to follow Him, and we'd never stray.
D
The only one who can mess up is me.
G
None of you can change my destiny.
D
I'm headed for that mansion there on high,
        A   D
And I'll reach it by and by.

HE'S MY KEEPER

1.
  D   D7
When the storms of life assail me,
        G   D
When I'm lost and can't find my way,
      G   D
I've an anchor who has never failed me,
       E   A
And it holds me steadfast in the way.
            D
Though all others say I'll never make it,
      G   D
I look to Jesus, and when I see Him,
      G   D
I know I'll not only make it but victoriously,
           A   D
And through Him, I will win.

Chorus
  D   G   D
He's my keeper when I walk through troubled waters.
       E   A
He's my staff at the end of the day.
  G   D
He said He'd never ever leave me
      E   A
But go with me all of the way.

Carol J. Hill Chatman

```
        D                          D7
He's my Alpha, Omega, beginning and end,
        G
My Protector, Savior, Counselor, and Friend.
        D
My father, my mother, He said He would be.
                  A         D
He's everything, everything to me.


2.
  D                    D7
He's the captain of my salvation,
          G            D
Guides my ship on life's troubled seas.
      G          D
When I'm overwhelmed, He's standing close,
            E                  A
And He knows when I'm brought to my knees.
      D
When all has failed each way I turn,
      G              D
It's then I give it up in His hands.
      G              D
As He stills the waves, and I see the shore,
        A    D
I'm at peace again.
```

My God Can Deliver

OH, BE CAREFUL, LITTLE CHILDREN

1.
A   D   A
As in days long ago, when Mom washed us each one
                 B   E
And put on us garments so fair,
           A   D   A
She would tell us, "Be careful. Don't get dirty just now.
           E   A
We're waiting to go over there."

Chorus
A   D   A
Oh, be careful, little children, as you're wandering below,
                  B   E
That you don't stain your robes of pure white.
    A
Oh, be careful, little children,
      D   A
For the Lord's cleaned every spot,
        E   A
Made us ready for our heavenly flight.

2.
 A   D   A
How tempted we were, with each mudhole we saw,
         B   E
To let down our guard for some fun.

Carol J. Hill Chatman

```
        A                    D         A
But then we'd remember Mother's words once again:
                  E         A
"You can't go if you're not ready, son."


3.
   A                     D        A
Mom no longer guides me; I'm all on my own.
            B         E
But the Spirit of God lets me know
      A              D         A
That if I make heaven, I must hear His voice,
                  E         A
When He speaks, and the answer is no.


4.
A                           D         A
I'm still tempted when others say, "See how much fun.
          B       E
Just try it, and see if I'm right."
           A                    D         A
But the angels watch o'er me, and I stand tall and straight;
              E         A
I won't stain my garments so white.
```

My God Can Deliver

IN A MILLION YEARS

1.
    G
In a million years I'll stand around

The throne of God up there.
    C
I'll tell how He delivered me
                G
In answer to my prayer.

When the road was rough, and the way seemed long,
                      C
He gave me the victory.
                      G
So by His grace I'll run this race;
          D   G
I wouldn't trade it in a million years.

Chorus
    C
In a million years I'll brag about
    G
The battles I face today.

How God was there, and Satan had to flee.
         A   D
Wouldn't have it any other way.

    G
With those who've gone before me,
                              C
Who have fought through blood and tears,
                             G
I'll shout His praise through the endless days.
           D   G
I wouldn't trade it in a million years.

2.
    G
I've fought the fight, I've kept the faith,

I've shed a lot of tears.
C
I've fought the devil on his own turf,
                  G
And in Jesus's name endured.

So some day in heaven I'll say,
           C
"His promises are secure."
        G
I'll be so glad I kept the faith.
       D   G
I wouldn't trade it in a million years.

My God Can Deliver

LET HIM WALK UPON YOUR WATERS

1.
G
Jesus instructed His disciples

To cross over to Bethsaida,
                                D
And He'd meet them over on the other side.

But as they were crossing,

The waves began their crashing,
                                G
And none of their efforts made the waves subside.

It was after midnight—

Nothing now could save them;

Their strength was gone,
                C
And they were in despair.
    D
As they looked out they saw Him,

There upon the waters,
                G
Walking on the water to them there.

Carol J. Hill Chatman

Chorus
   G
Let Him walk upon your waters that are troubled.
                        D
Let Him say, "Peace be still."

Let Him calm the howling storms

That are raging all around you,
                               G
And you'll see them subject to the Master's will.

Though it seems your boat is filling

With waves and waves of trouble,
                        C
And all your effort brings you is despair,
   D
Just remember He's the Master,

Who can calm the waters.
                           G
Look up, and you will find Him walking there.

2.
   G
I remember Paul and Silas

As they were beaten
                    D
And taken to the prison—both in chains.

The devil must have thought

That since He had them captive,

                                      G
Surely they'd no longer call His name.

But within the prison

They began their singing,
                                   C
Praising God they'd suffered for His name.
    D
And at the name of Jesus,

All the bands were broken.
                                  G
The devil knew his efforts were in vain.

GOD, YOU SO LOVED

1.
  G   D   G
God, You so loved this world that You made
        C   G
And gave it unto man.
       C   G
And though we've failed so terribly,
      A   D
We're still a part of Your plan.
      G
You could have wiped the slate clean
    C   D
And started all over again.
    C   G
But because of Your great love for me,
    D   G
You had another plan.

First Chorus
    C   G
How very much this love cost You
        D   G
Because of this other plan.

My God Can Deliver

2.
    G   D   G
I marvel at all the things You've made
      C   G
And know it was for me
     C   G
That You endured the rugged cross,
    A   D
And hung on Calvary.
        G
There's nothing I can compare this love to;
    C   D
It's so hard to understand
   C   G
Because there's no greater love in this world
        D   G
Than the love You have for man.

Second Chorus
C   G
Oh, how great the cost to You
        D   G
Because of Your love for man.

I JUST LOVE TO SIT

1.
C F
I love just to sit
  C
Here in His presence,
 G
Lifting my voice
    C
In praise unto Him.

2.
   F
I love just to sit
  C
Quietly before Him,
 G
Feeling His touch
      C
Again and again.

WE HAVE POWER O'ER THE ENEMY

1.
G
We have power o'er all power of the enemy.
                                        C
We have power to rebuke in Jesus's name.

We have power o'er all power of the enemy,
                                       G
And he has to flee, the Word of God proclaims.

2.
G
So like soldiers, we are all prepared for battle,
                           C
All in battle garments white arrayed.
                                  G
For the battle is not ours that waits before us;
       D   G
We just have to speak the Word in Jesus's name.

Carol J. Hill Chatman

IT WON'T BE LONG NOW

1.
  A
This world is rocking and reeling
        D   A
For that day of sweet release.

When all the wars have ended,
         B   E
No more blood will stain her face.
    A
The sin and sorrow, pain and death,
   D   A
Have all been left behind,

And we're living in God's paradise
    E   A
Beyond the realm of time.

Chorus
A
It won't be long now
         D   A
Till we'll be walking streets of gold.

It won't be long now;
     B   E
I can feel it in my soul.

       A
It won't be long now
          D   A
Till He'll be coming back again,
     D   A
And everything will be all right
       E   A
When we go home with Him.

2.
A
You see a little one in pain
    D   A
And have to wonder why.

And others with no one to care
    B   E
If they should live or die.
  A
It breaks our hearts and makes us weep
    D   A
For we can't understand.

But we know everything will be all right
     E   A
When we go home with Him.

3.
A
He said when He went away
      D   A
He'd be coming back again.

He'd go prepare a place for us,
     B   E
Where there will be no sin.

Carol J. Hill Chatman

    A
There'll be no heartache anymore,
    D   A
No reason then to cry.

A place with God the Father,
  E   A
Up there in the sky.

INCLUDE ME

1.
  D
My friends don't understand me;
     G   D
They say I'm not the same.
     A
And then I try to tell them
       G   D
How my life has all been changed.

If they could only know the peace
    G
And joy that came to me
   D
Since I received an offer
      A   D
That changed my destiny. So—

Chorus
   G
Include me when you're gathering
       D
Round the table of the Lord!
     A
I've received my invitation;
      D
I've been bought back by His blood.

Carol J. Hill Chatman

    G
I have made my preparations,
      D
And I'm ready now to go.
    A
So include me in the number
          D
Of people you will know.

2.
D
You will see me in that number
      G   D
Gathered round the throne up there.
        A
And you'll hear me shouting, "Glory!"
     G   D
As a robe of white I'll wear.

The world holds no attraction;
      G
I've been born again, you see.
      D
And my eyes are on the future
  A   D
My God's prepared for me. So—

3.
   D
I have so many loved ones
    G
Who say, "I think I'll wait,
   A
And after I have lived it up,
   G   D
I'll step inside the gate."

No promise of tomorrow,
    G
No peace of God today,
    D
Their borrowed time is running out—
  A   D
It soon will be too late. But—

THERE IS ROOM

1.
    C   F   C
When we enter God's house, let's remember
        G   C
That a table has been spread where all can be fed.
          F   C
And everything we need is on that table,
       G   C
And a place already set for you and me.

Chorus
    C   F   C
And there is room at the Master's table.
        G   C
And there's water from the well that never shall run dry.
         F   C
And there is meat to feed the hungry.
       G   C
And living water that will satisfy.

2.
    C   F   C
When Moses was leading God's children,
        G   C
The manna would fall; there was enough for all.

```
         F                  C
```
Like Israel, we can't store for tomorrow.
```
  G                       C
```
Every day we need a fresh supply.

3.
```
      C       F     C
```
I remember the story of Daniel,
```
    G           C
```
Who refused to eat all the old king's meat.
```
         F             C
```
He was eating at a different table—
```
     G                    C
```
The table that gives us our supply.

IF YOU'RE LIVING JUST FOR THINGS

1.
```
G                    D              G
```
If you're living just for things, they soon will vanish.
```
              D                 G
```
If you're living just for gold, it fades away.
```
            C                       G
```
If you're living for life's goods, they all will tarnish,
```
       A                      D
```
And with the passing moments, they decay. So—

Chorus
```
         C                  G
```
I'm living, and I'm banking on my future.
```
         D                      G
```
I'm preparing for a life that's free from pain.
```
           C                    G
```
And I'm giving all the things that really matter
```
       A                  D
```
And receiving back to me tenfold again.
```
       G           D           G
```
I'm giving smiles and words that will encourage,
```
          D                 G
```
And I'll try to help in every way I can.
```
         C                   G
```
I am making big investments in my future
```
                  D            G
```
In God's tried and proven life assurance plan.

2.
```
      G           D          G
I'm building on the Rock of my salvation.
      D                          G
I'm building on the things I'm sure will stand
            C                    G
'Cause I'm using a tried-and-proven blueprint,
         A                  D
And my Architect has only proven plans. So—
```

KEEPER OF THE DOOR

Chorus
```
   C                            F
Lord, You're the keeper of the door;
             G         C
Your name's the password to get in.
                            F
There's no other way to enter there,
         G        C
No other sacrifice for sin.
                           F
Lord, You're the keeper of the door,
        G           C
And we have to come by You.
                  F
If we enter heaven's gate,
              G         C
We'll find no other name will do.
```

1.
```
   C      F              C
You said to come and let us reason together.
              F                 C
You said to come and try You, and we'd see.
              F                 C
You know there are so many voices calling,
        F       G           C
Help us choose the path that leads to Thee.
```

My God Can Deliver

2.
```
      F                      C
So many doors for me are now open.
         F                 C
So many paths that I alone can choose.
             F                      C
How much I need your steady hand to guide me,
       F          G          C
All my future molded by the way I choose.
```

Carol J. Hill Chatman

A PRESENT HELP

Chorus
  A   D
He's a mighty present help in the time of trouble.
      A   E
He's a mighty present help in the midst of life's storms.
     A   D
He's a mighty present help when we feel our weakest,
  A   E   A
And that's when He carries us, safe in His arms.

1.
  A
When the winds of life are blowing,
     D
And it seems our ship is sinking,
        A
And the waves are rising higher,
            E
All hope is almost gone.
    A
It's then we see the Master,
     D   A
Walking to us on the waters.

The waves are looking calmer;
      E   A
We know we're not alone.

2.
  A
When we're crushed beneath a burden
        D
That's too heavy to carry,
       A
And we dread to face tomorrow—
              E
It's just more of today—
   A
It's then we remember
       D   A
That He said He'd never leave us.

He walks before us
    E   A
To open up the way.

HOW MANY TIMES?

1.
C
Just like a sheep, I was wandering lost,
F　　　　　　C
Far from the Father's care.
　　F　　　　　　　　C
The pastures were green, the sun shining bright;
　D　　　　　G
I hadn't a worry or care.
C
Jesus spoke then, I barely could hear;
　　　F　　　　　　C
My attention was far, far away.
　　F　　　　　C
I didn't say no, but I didn't say yes.
　　　　　　　G　　　C
I'll think on it more someday.

Chorus
　C
How many? How many? How many times
　　　　　　F　　　　C
Have You tried to rescue me?
　F　　　　　　　　C
How many? How many? How many times
　　　　　D　　　　　G
Has Your Spirit spoken to me?

My God Can Deliver

```
        C
How many? How many? How many times
            F                C
Have You found me all dirty and cold?
     F         C
Lord, once again, please ask me in,
                    G         C
To the safety and peace of Your fold.


On Final Chorus add
        F          C
Before it's too late, please ask me in,
                    G         C
To the safety and peace of your fold.


2.
C
Later along in the bustle of life,
       F            C
I heard a more urgent plea.
            F            C
I sensed Jesus say, "Before it's too late,
     D                    G
Won't you please listen to Me?"
         C
But things were so busy there in my prime—
  F                C
Too many things in my way—
      F                C
Those were the words I spoke to Him then,
                G        C
And turned and went on my way.
```

74 *Carol J. Hill Chatman*

3.
```
   C
Still later on life has slowed down,
         F              C
But it seems I'm too busy to care.
         F             C
"He must have forgotten about me," I say,
     D         G
As I sit alone in my chair.
     C
"Why doesn't He speak to me once again,
       F          C
As He did long, long ago."
          F              C
Then I hear in my heart, *I've tried and I've tried,*
              G         C
```
But always your answer was no.

COME, CARRY MY CROSS

1.
     C   F   C
The cross was so heavy that Jesus bore that day.
   G   C
My sins on His back, and the cross starts to sway.
                   F   C
They call for Simon to lighten His load;
   G   C-C7
I still hear Him calling on that Calvary road.

Chorus
    C   F   C
Come carry my cross up Golgotha's Hill.
          G   C
Can't you picture Him there on the cross calling still.
              F   C
I'll carry your sins and your shame.

Don't you see?
   G   C
If only you'll carry, my cross for Me.

2.
    C   F   C
Sometimes the way gets so weary and long
   G   C
That I lose my joy, and I lose my song.

Carol J. Hill Chatman

     F C
Then once again I picture dark Calvary,
    G   C-C7
And I say, "Yes, Lord, I'll carry Your cross with me."

3.
   C   F C
I'm climbing my last mountain on my way home.
   G
I can hear loved ones cheering from there
     C
Round the throne.
      F C
I know I'll be so happy on that last day
   G   C-C7
That I carried the cross of the Lord on my way.

My God Can Deliver

TRASH CAN

1.
     C   F   C
Our ears are all bombarded with vulgarities today.
                                  D   G
They say we're just enlightened in a different sort of way.
               C
The things that are pure and sacred
    F   C
Are often laughed about.
                            G   C
We'll find what's really garbage when Jesus sweeps us out.

Chorus
     C   F   C
My ears are not a trash can that the devil spits into.
                                      G
My eyes have seen the great things that my Lord can do.
    C
My feet have walked on holy ground,
  F   C
So I can sing and shout.

I am a temple of the Lord;
    C   C
His glory is all about.

2.
```
     C                             F                C
```
David said, "I'll not set before me things that will defile."
```
                                 D             G
```
I am a temple of the Lord, and I am His own child,
```
     C                               F         C
```
My eyes were really made to view the beauty all about.
```
                                 G              C
```
I refuse to allow old Satan to shut the good things out.

3.
```
        C                         F                 C
```
You see, I can hardly wait to walk those streets of gold,
```
                                D           G
```
To look upon my mansion, to feast my hungry soul.
```
     C                             F           C
```
To listen to the angel choir and then to join that band.
```
                                G             C
```
There'll be no contamination of the devil in that land.

THE LORD REIGNETH

Psalm 93:1
  G
The Lord reigneth;
  C   G
He is clothed with majesty.
      C   G
The Lord is clothed with strength
            D
Wherewith He hath girded Himself.

Psalm 96:10
  G
Say among the heathen
        C   G
That the Lord reigneth.
      C   G
The world ... shall be established
       D   G
That it shall not be moved.

Psalm 97:1
G
The Lord reigneth:
C   G
Let the earth rejoice.

```
      C           G
Let the multitude of isles
      D
Be glad thereof.


Psalm 99:1
      G
The Lord reigneth:
C           G
Let the people tremble.
      C           G
He sitteth between the cherubims.
            D     G
Let the earth be moved.
      C           G
He sitteth between the cherubims.
            D     G
Let the earth be moved.
```

JESUS, JESUS

1.
  G   C
One day by the wayside a blind beggar sat
                        G   D
As the crowds following Jesus were passing by.
      G   C
The beggar cried out, "What doth this mean?"
                G   D   G
"A man called Jesus," was their reply.

Chorus
G   C   G
Jesus, Jesus came down from heaven
          D
To set men free.
G   C   G   D   G
Jesus, Jesus, Jesus, have mercy on me.

2.
  G   C
Here so much later, my life wrecked by sin,
           G   D
I knew that I would one day have to die.
G   C
I had no hope, no peace within.
                  G   D   G
Then came the whisper, "The Lord's passing by."

Carol J. Hill Chatman

3.
```
    G                         C
If you've lost your way, and you're bound by sin,
            G               D
Please let me tell you what you can do.
  G                   C
Call to the Master; He wants to come in.
                G     D     G
He's never too busy to listen to you.
```

LORD, GUIDE MY FOOTSTEPS

1.
  D   G
Lord, when I look over my shoulder,
  D   A
I see others there behind.
  D   G
Let my footsteps light their pathway
  D   A   D
So that in heaven, as bright lights they'll shine.

Chorus
  D   G
Lord, guide my footsteps from here to heaven,
  D   A
So those that follow can find the way.
  D   G
If there be little ones walking behind me,
  D   A   D
Lord, guide my footsteps; don't let me stray.

2.
  D   G
Jesus taught if salt has lost its savor,
      D   A
It's useful for nothing but to cast away.

Carol J. Hill Chatman

    D   G
And if our light be under a bushel,
D   A   D
No one can see it in this dark day.

JESUS IS CALLING

1.
  G
Once again now, you've made your way
                            D
To the house of the Lord, that's true.

And as you've sat here, the Spirit's been calling;
                        G
He's been calling for you.

Chorus (with echo)
  C   G
Je - - - - sus is call - - - - ing
(Jesus is calling.)   (Jesus is calling.)
    D   G
Is call - - - - - - - ing for you.
    (calling for you)   (calling for you).
  C   G
Je - - - - sus is call - - - - ing
(Jesus is calling)   (Jesus is calling),
     D   G
He's call - - - - - - ing for you.
     (Yes, He is calling)   (calling for you).

Carol J. Hill Chatman

2.
G
But you've said, "Lord, I'll just wait
                            D
Till my life's almost through.

Then I'll come back and go down,
                        G
And give my heart to You."

3.
G
As you walk out this very night,
                                D
While the Spirit is pleading with you,

You may be saying your very last no
                           G
To God who's calling for you.

LOVE

1.
   A
Love always gives, never takes,

Always mends, never breaks,
                                 E
Always ready to go the second mile.

Love is reaching out to you

To see what it can do
                              A
To make you happy and to see you smile.

If you turn that love away,

It will be a gloomy day,
                           D
And Satan will be really on your track.

So won't you be real smart,
     A
And give God's love a start,
    E   A
And let Him lead you gently, safely back?

Chorus
```
   E                A
Back to the arms of Jesus,
   E                A
Back to the Master's hold;
   D              A
Back to peace and contentment,
   E                    A
Back to the safety of the fold.
```

2.
```
    A
The enemy comes but for to steal,

Never help or never heal.
                              E
He comes for nothing but to tear you down.

He will take your smile away,

Usher in a gloomy day,
                              A
And before you know it, he will have you bound.

Turn to Jesus right today.

Let Him take those chains away
                              D
And secure for you a place on higher ground.

Can't you hear Him call?
        A
Please make Him Lord of all,
        E                     A
And He will surely turn your life around.
```

JESUS, I'VE SAT ON YOUR DOORSTEP

1.
D   G   D
Every battle in life that I'm faced with
                        A
Seems so hopeless when I face it alone.
    G   D
My problems don't have any answers
               A   D
Till I bring them to God at the throne.

Chorus
        G   D
Jesus, I've sat on Your doorstep so often,
               A
Asking for directions in life.
       G   D
Jesus, I've sat on Your doorstep so often,
        A   D
Asking Your will for my life.

2.
   D   G   D
When life doesn't have any answers,
              A
And my steps seem so in vain,

Carol J. Hill Chatman

```
      G                D
Then I turn down Your path, Jesus,
              A           D
And You'll hear me calling Your name.


3.
         D       G     D
The mountaintop seems so far away
                         A
And the valley so filled with despair.
         G              D
Then I notice the lilies are blooming
                    A       D
And know that You placed them there.
```

DEAR LORD

A
Let everywhere I go, dear Lord,

And everything I do, dear Lord,
                              E
And every step I make just follow You.

Let every word I speak, dear Lord,

And every thought I think, dear Lord,
                                    A
And every way I look, God, honor You.

Let all my ways and actions, Lord,

And all my selfish thoughts, dear God,
                              D
Be burned out, so You can shine anew.

      E
And everyone I meet, dear God,

Will not be meeting me,
                              A
Will not be meeting me but meeting You.

  E
Will not be meeting me,

Will not be meeting me,
                                        A
Will not be meeting me but meeting You.

MY THOUGHTS ON EVOLUTION

1.
D
I think that man,
G
In his desperation
    A
To try and find out how
      G   D
And why he came to be,

Completely ignoring God,
  G
Who has all the answers,
  A
Tries to keep man swinging by his tail
                D
Up in our family tree.

Chorus
(Spoken): So while they keep trying to figure it all out,
        G
I'm gonna walk down by that river,
      D
Put my feet down in that water,
  A   D
Lift my hands in singing, "Hallelujah to the Lamb!"
        G
I'm gonna visit all those loved ones

      D
Who have walked this road before me,
  A
And join in their praises
          D
To the great I Am.

2.
 D
They say an explosion
G
Put this world together
A
And formed the flowers
    G   D
And put the trees in place.

I say the mighty voice of God—
   G
Sounding like thunder—
  A
Spoke the words that
          D
Formed this human race.

3.
 D
Seems our generation,
   G
Like in the days of Noah,
 A
Have shut their doors to God,
    G   D
So He can't see their sin.

But in Noah's day,

      G
It was God who did the shutting.
      A
With believers on the inside,
                   D
He's gonna shut those doors again.

HE'S NO LONGER IN THE MANGER

1.
  A
He's no longer in the manger;
        D   A
Wise men cannot find Him there.

He's no longer at the temple
        B   E
That He pronounced the House of Prayer.
                        A
You won't find Him at that garden,
       D   A
Where He prayed so long ago.

Nor at the Hall of Pilate,
      E   A
Where the soldiers beat Him so.

Chorus
      D
For He is risen; He is risen.
  A
Now He's sitting on His throne,
         E
And He rules from heaven,
              A
Ever watching o'er His own.

    D
He is risen; He is risen.
  A
King of Kings and Lord is He.
                E
Soon He's coming back in glory—
                  A
Yes, He's coming back for me.

2.
  A
Nor could the cruel cross hold Him;
     D   A
He's no longer there today.

When they railed and spat upon Him,
    B   E
The sun just fled away.
                A
Then the dark clouds and the thunder
     D   A
And an earthquake at that site

Made the soldiers who were witnesses
        E   A
Say, "We've killed our Lord this night."

3.
  A
You won't find Him on the hillside
    D
In that land so far away

You won't find Him at the grave site
    B   E
For He rose on that third day.

```
                          A
But you'll find Him—yes, you'll find Him—
       D           A
When you call His name in prayer.

You will find Him—yes, you'll find Him—
         E           A
He'll be waiting for you there.
```

HE WALKS THE MOUNTAINTOPS

1.
C
I see storm clouds gathering.
    F   C
The time of the harvest
    F   C
Could be any day now;
        G
The fields are white.
  C
Jerusalem has gathered
    F   C
Her sons and her daughters.
    F   C
The earth now stands ready.
    F   C
The King now stands ready.
    F   C
His bride now stands ready
  G   C
For taking her flight.

Chorus
C
He walks the mountaintops.
 F   C
He's in the valleys.

Carol J. Hill Chatman

```
     F            C
And when the storm rages,
 D         G
He calms my soul.
      C
Wherever He leads me,
  F         C
He's already walked there.
      F         C
So why should I fear
        G       C
When God's in control.
```

2.
```
      C
I remember the promise
          F     C
Jesus made His disciples—
      F      C
That if He went away,
                G
He would come again.
        C
He'd send back the Spirit
      F     C
To guide us in all truth.
      F         C
We would receive power;
      F         C
We would be His witnesses.
      F         C
And when all had heard,
           G         C
He said he would come again!
```

3.
C
Jesus said that someday
     F   C
All wars will be ended.
        F   C
There'll be no more heartache.
           G
All trouble will end.
    C
He'll reign in Jerusalem.
  F   C
Truth will be exalted,
  F   C
Righteousness the order.
  F   C
Peace like a river
     G   C
Will flow among men!

I FEEL RESTORATION COMING ON

1.
C
Adam, in the garden,
     F   C
He surely lost our deed.

He gave place to the devil
     D   G
For things he didn't need.
C
Jesus came to buy back
   F
All Adam lost that day.
C   G   C
I feel restoration coming on.

Chorus
C   F   C
I feel restoration coming on.
      F   C
I feel restoration coming on.

God sent out His singers
    F
And gave to them a song,
     C   G   C
Saying, "I feel restoration coming on."

2.
C
What the cankerworm hath eaten,
   F   C
God said He would restore.

What the enemy hath stolen
        D   G
Will return to us once more.
      C
Our seeds that we have planted
     F
Will flourish at last.
C   G   C
I feel restoration coming on.

3.
The end time is upon us.
        F   C
What we do, we must do fast

To gather in the harvest
    D   G
Before the winter blast.
C
God has promised plenty,
   F
If we'll bring in the grain.
C   G   C
I feel restoration coming on.

COUNT ME IN

1.
  D
I received my invitation
        G
And sent back my acceptance,
     A
Saying, "Yes, I'll be there
      G   D
When the marriage feast is spread.

I've rearranged my schedule,
      G
Making sure that I'll not miss it.
    A
I want to sit around that table
      G   D
As the Master breaks the bread."

Chorus
  D   G
Count me in when you're sitting
       D
Round the throne up there in heaven,
     A
And the angel choir is singing,
    D
"Hallelujah to the Lamb!"

      G
Count me in when the Master
           D
Breaks the bread around that table,
      A
And the marriage feast is ready.
           D
You can surely count me in.

2.
  D
When I first received the call
      G
From the Holy of Holies, saying that
A
There was a place reserved,
  G   D
Wouldn't I please attend?

I began to take the time,
      G
Making sure that I'd be ready.
A
I have this feeling that
     G   D
I won't get this chance again.

3.
    D
I can feel the tug from heaven
    G
As I see that day approaching.
     A
The bridegroom soon is coming
    G   D
To take us home with Him.

What a jubilation,
     G
Seeing all those gone before us.
  A
What anticipation
      G   D
As we suddenly ascend.

HELP, I NEED GRACE

1.
A
I called up this morning
     D   A
And laid my heart bare.

I said, "Lord, I know
   B   E
You always hear my prayers.
   A
I'm really in a mess this time.
  D
I'm afraid I need Your grace.
    A
Could You ship out a big supply?
     E   A
It could really save my face."

Chorus
A
I sent back the answer, Lord,
    D   A
That You just shipped to me.

The package that it came in
    B   E
Was much too small to be

Carol J. Hill Chatman

    A
The answer that I sought You for.
    D
I'm running out of time.
      A
Could You just send it COD,
    E   A
That answer that is mine?

2.
   A
I'm waiting for a notice
  D   A
To say it's on its way.

Just a note from heaven
       B   E
Would brighten up my day.
 A
So I fall down on my knees
     D
To get heaven on my line,
 A
And I'm told I just sent back
    E   A
The package that was mine.

3.
A
Lord, I really need to ask,
   D   A
"Do You give a guarantee

That tomorrow I won't be back
 B   E
Needing more for me?"

  A
Can't you see Jesus smiling
     D
Like something's on His mind
   A
Because He knows that I'll be back,
       E   A
Needing grace another time.

THE BATTLE IS THE LORD'S

I.
  G   C   G
When the enemy comes in like a flood,
                       A   D
I stand firm, covered by the blood.
                G   C
Through the battle heat, I strongly cry,
       G   D   G
"I have reinforcements from on high."

Chorus
     G
The battle is the Lord's.
    C
I am His; He is mine.
    G
The battle is the Lord's.
    A   D
He's there; He's on the front line.
     G
He walks ahead of me
      C
To give to me the victory.
     G
I'll never fear;
    D   G
The battle is the Lord's.

2.
```
G                         C          G
No weapon that's formed against me can stand.
                 A     D
I am safe in the Master's hand.
            G            C
When the angel of death is going by,
           G               D    G
The blood on the doorpost is my battle cry.
```

YOU CAN

1.
  G
Lord, we can't calm the waters

Of the raging seas.
  C
We can't put in the heart of man

What He needs to be.

Chorus
  G   D   G
You can. You can. Lord, You can.

2.
  G
We can't be the witness

That you'd have us to be.
  C
We can't understand our path,

So Lord, help us to see that …

3.
G
We can't understand tomorrow

Or know what it may bring.
C
But we know we trust it

To our heavenly King 'cause ...

4.
G
So I bring my problems

And lay them at your feet,
　C
Knowing I find answers there

That I could never see, but ...

Final Chorus
　G　　　D　　　G
You can. You can. Yes, You can.

THE BURDEN'S BEEN LIFTED

1
A
I've walked on the mountaintop,
  D
Been in the valleys,
        A   E
Where the load was too heavy to bear.
A   A7
Jesus was leading,
  D
But He hid His face.
    A   E   A
I cried out, "O God, are You there?"

Chorus
A   A7   D
The burden's been lifted, I've carried so long,
    A   E
That tried to bring me despair.
    A   D
The burden's been lifted; the enemy is gone.
    A   E   A
The armies of heaven are here.

2.
     A   A7
The skies were so dark.
     D
The fear of death
   A   E
Seemed to be hovering near.
   A   A7
I found no assurance
 D
Each way I turned.
     A   E   A
My heart was crushed to despair. But …

III.
   A   A7
So I march to the victory

That lies just ahead,
       A   E
Where faith has conquered my fears.
   A   A7
How sweet the miracle
 D
Jesus has wrought!
    A   E   A
The time for rejoicing is here.

4.
 A   A7
Now I see clearly
    D
The way up ahead.
    A   E
"The battle's been worth it," I say.

Carol J. Hill Chatman

  A
How sweet the victory
  D
Jesus has wrought.
    A   E   A
Souls in the balance are safe, so …

THE GIFT OF CHOICE

Chorus
G   C   G
It wasn't nails that held Him to that old rugged cross.
                     D   G
He could have called angels to descend.
               C   G
It wasn't nails that held Him to that old rugged cross.
            D   G
It was His awesome love He had for man.

1.
     G C   G
The scene on Golgotha's Hill that day
            D   G
Portrayed the heart of sinful man.
                    C   G
Such cruelty and anger against the Son of God
         D   G
Is hard for me to understand.

2.
  G   C G
When God sent to earth His only Son,
      D   G
It had to be; He had no other plan.

Carol J. Hill Chatman

```
              C     G
He knew when He gave us the precious gift to choose,
         D                   G
It put a powerful weapon in our hand.
```

I'VE GOT THE ATTRIBUTES OF GOD

1.
   D   G   A
I've got the attributes of God, my Father,
                            D
And I'm growing every day.
                      G
I want others when they see me
      A   D
To recognize Him right away.

2.
   D   G   A
I've got the attributes of God, my Father.
                         D
Let His compassion show in me.
                      G
Let there be no misunderstanding
    A   D
Of my Father's claim on me.

3.
   D   G   A
I've got the attributes of God, my Father.
                        D
I try to follow close behind.

Carol J. Hill Chatman

                              G
Though the example's hard to follow,
      A   D
I am His, and He is mine!

MIGHTY MAN

1.
 G
Gideon took his men by night

And tore Baal's groves all down,
   C
Knowing this would cause a stir
           D
All around the town.
   C   D
"Let him die!" they all cried.
    C   D
His father said, "Not true!

If Baal can't defend himself,
               G
He surely can't help you."

Chorus
  G
Mighty man of valor,

Hiding from the enemy,
  C
Don't you know that God is God
               D
Who came to set you free?

Carol J. Hill Chatman

```
  C              D
Go tear down the altars
      C          D
Your father built to Baal.

Build one to Jehovah,
                G
The God that never fails.


2.
  G
Gideon took his army,

Soldiers big and strong.
  C
God gave the instructions
                   D
For the fearful to go home.
      C          D
He said to take the others
      C              D
Down to the water and see.

Those who watched while drinking
                 G
His army that would be.


3.
G
I have built my altars

Of vanity and pride.
      C
And then I've closed and locked the doors,
              D
So no one sees inside.
```

My God Can Deliver

>   C   D
> I feel the Spirit tugging,
>   C   D
> Saying He wants to set me free.
>
> What a mighty man of valor
>   G
> God wants me to be.

STAINS

1.
    F   C
A woman one day was thrust at His feet.
                            F
"She should be stoned," they said.
                          C
Jesus knelt down and wrote on the ground.
                           F
Her hecklers then all turned away.

Chorus
  B♭   F
Wash me, and I shall be whiter than snow,
  C   F
Whiter than snow, whiter than snow.
    B♭   F
No matter how many stains on my name,
C   F
I shall be whiter than snow.

2.
F   C
No fuller can wash the stains that I've made.
                  F
I've drifted so far, far astray.

                                    C
Then the voice of Jesus calls softly to me.
                              F
That He died just to take them away.

3.
    F   C
"My burden's so heavy; my load seems too much.
                 F
I cannot bear it," I say.
                       C
Then I hear Jesus, and I feel His touch.
              F
I kneel at the altar to pray.

4.
  F   C
My name to Him is now snowy-white.
          F
No fault in me He sees.
                     C
My fellow man may still see my faults,
                      F
But His righteousness covers me.

HE'S ALPHA AND OMEGA

1.
    D
The blind man sitting by the way

Had no idea today
 G
He'd meet someone in the crowd
                         D
Who would change his night to day.

As he heard Jesus going by,
          G
He began to plead,
      D
"Jesus, Son of David,
    A   D
Have mercy on me."

Chorus
    A
He's Alpha and Omega,
     G   D
The beginning and the end.
    A
The bread sent down from heaven
    E   A
That feeds the soul of man.

      D
The great Jehovah, living God,
         G
Master, Savior too.
           D
Anything too hard for you
   A   D
Is something He can do.

2.
    D
The crowd showed no mercy.

They warned him to be quiet,
   G
But he cried out all the more
             D
Till Jesus saw his plight.

When Jesus stopped to talk with him,
             G
He asked what He could do.

The blind man pleaded for his sight.
       A   D
He received sight and forgiveness, too.

Carol J. Hill Chatman

A COUNTER OF MINUTES

A mother's time is always in minutes.
How she finds so many is a mystery to me.
Seems there's always a minute for everything,
And each thing done to a T:

    A minute to cook up the breakfast,
    A minute to make up the bed,
    A minute to dress little Suzie,
    A minute to comb a bedraggled head.

    A minute to make jams and jellies,
    A minute to mop up a mess,
    A minute to fix broken toys,
    A minute to make Mary's dress.

    A minute to polish the silver,
    A minute to vacuum the rug,
    A minute to wash all the dishes,
    A minute to clean out the tub.

    A minute to do the dusting,
    A minute to hang out the clothes,
    A minute to do all the mending,
    A minute to doctor hurt toes.

    A minute to pick up the laundry,
    A minute to sort it and wash,
    A minute to change all the linen,
    A minute to can all the squash.

A minute to take out the garbage,
A minute to beat all the rugs,
A minute to help with the lessons,
A minute to give each one a hug.

A minute to shine all the windows,
A minute to wax all the floors,
A minute to make something special,
A minute to help with the chores.

A minute to clear off the table,
A minute to mow all the lawn,
A minute to write loved ones a letter,
A minute for having some fun.

All the things Mom can pack in a minute—
It's fun to just watch her and see.
I can just hope I'm as successful
When the counter of minutes is me.

Carol J. Hill Chatman

CHRIS'S LETTER TO GOD

Dear God,

1.
  C   G
God, watch over Daddy and keep him, I pray,
                              C
For Mom and I need him to hold us today.
                                F
I've seen Mommy crying, and I've heard her say,
       C   G   C
"God, watch over Daddy; please keep him, I pray."

2.
      C   G
I've seen Mommy crying as she tucked me in bed.
                          C
I've heard her praying—the things that she said.
                          F
The seeds Daddy's sowing, he'll reap them someday,
    C   G   C
So watch over Daddy, and keep him, I pray.

3.
     C   G
Tell Daddy I'm growing; I'll soon be quite tall.
                        C
I need him for guidance 'cause I am so small.

```
                        F
I know Mommy's doing the best that she can,
      C                      G       C
But we need my Daddy; sure, You understand.


4.
  C                   G
God, if You ever hear little boys pray,
                         C
Please hear my crying and answer today.
                        F
Give Daddy the courage to be a big man,
         C                    G       C
And bring him home to me as soon as you can.

                         F
                        Love,
                         C
                        Chris
```

Carol J. Hill Chatman

PROBLEM SOLVER

1.
   A
So many answers have been found
            E
Here on my knees.

So many problems have melted down
           A
Here on my knees.

So many burdens have rolled away.
           D
My heart's been lifted up today
    E
As before the Lord I stay
        A
Down on my knees.

2.
   A
The day is brighter when I start
         E
Down on my knees.

Satan's attacks just fall apart
       A
Down on my knees.

The heavy yoke he'd make me bear
        D
Seems to slip off, I do declare,
        E
And I never have a care
        A
Here on my knees.

3.
  A
Would you like to try it, friend,
        E
Down on your knees?

There's a peace that never ends
        A
Down on your knees.

If your load seems hard to bear,
      D
Jesus said to leave it there.
      E
And this joy you can share
       A
Down on your knees.

I'LL BE LOOKING FOR HIM IN THE MORNING

1.
   A
When I enter that beautiful city,
                         E
Oh, the sights that my eyes shall behold!
     A
I will look on the walls made of jasper,
                  E   A
And walk on those streets made of gold.

Chorus
       D   A
I'll be looking for Him in the morning;
                    E
I'll be looking for Jesus at noon.
      A
By the signs in His Word He has given,
           E   A
I know that His coming is soon.

2.
    A
I'll see Abraham, Isaac, and Jacob—
                      E
And all those who've gone on before.

       A
Then my eyes shall behold my Savior
              E   A
When I step on that heavenly shore.

3.
 A
Will I see you there that first morning,
                     E
Just after the Bride takes her flight?
      A
Will you walk with me down by that river,
       E   A
That beautiful river of life?

I'VE GOT THAT OLD-TIME RELIGION IN MY SOUL

(Lyrics by Rebecca Hill Toland/Music by Calverine McLaughlin Hill)

Chorus
```
      C                    F         C
I've got that old-time religion in my soul;
                                    G
The kind that lifts me up and makes me whole.
              C
Now I can pray and sing and shout,
              F           C
Because my Lord has lifted me out;
                   G         C
I've got that old-time religion in my soul.
```

1.
```
  C
He lifts me up when I am down,
          F              C
And plants my feet on the solid ground;

He pulls my soul from the miry clay,
           D              G
And stands me on God's Rock to stay.
     C
Hallelujah! I am free
```

My God Can Deliver

```
           F              C
Because my Jesus has saved me!
                    G         C
I've got that old-time religion in my soul.


2.
C
He saved my soul from a burning hell,
            F              C
And gave me joy like a ringing bell;

He gave me a peace down in my heart,
         D         G
And from His love I'll never part.
     C
Hallelujah! I am free
           F              C
Because my Jesus has saved me!
                    G         C
I've got that old-time religion in my soul.
```

Carol J. Hill Chatman

WHAT WILL YOUR ANSWER BE?

1.
     D   G   D
While walking along on this road of life,
                         A
Our hearts are corrupted by sin.
 D   G   D
Jesus says to come, let Him make you anew.
              A   D
What will be your answer to Him?

Chorus
  G   D
What will you say? What will your answer be
   E   A
When Jesus calls you home?
 D   G   D
When He so tenderly deals with your heart,
        A   D
But you say, "Leave me alone"?

2.
D   G   D
Others have walked this road that you trod,
            A
Denying that God ever lived.

```
       D              G    D
The rich man said as he burned in hell,
                 A      D
"Send Lazarus; tell others you live."
```

3.
```
       D            G        D
If you reject His death on the cross,
                      A
And count it as nothing today,
       D                    G      D
You'll stand before Him at the end of this road.
               A      D
What will you then have to say?
```

JESUS ON MY SIDE

1.
  A   D   A
Though there are problems and troubles around me—
                                     E
Seems like I'm pressed from without and within—
A   D   A
Jesus has said He'll never forsake me.
                        E   A
Through His sweet name, I can't help but win.

Chorus
A   D   A
Jesus on my side, and that makes a majority.
                        E
Jesus on my side, and I cannot fail.
  A   D   A
Though all hell is standing against me,
           E   A
With Jesus on my side, all is well.

2.
A   D   A
We know the coming of Jesus is nearing;
                 E
I feel the presence of Satan so strong.

   A   D   A
Now is surely the time to look upward.
                                E   A
We'll leave this old world, singing this song.

TOO LATE

Chorus
   D   A
Too late, the trumpet has blown.
   E   A
Too late, He's come for His own.
   D   A
Too late to kneel down and pray.
         E   A
For I've waited, I've waited, I've waited too late.

1.
     A   E
The door fast is closing; the end is so nigh
        D   A   E
When Jesus is coming from His home on high.
    A   D
He said to be ready if we would go in.
              A   E   A
Here's what you'll hear if you miss it, my friend:

2.
    A   E
His hands are stretched out now; He's waiting for you.
     D   A   E
Can't you hear him calling? What more can He do?

    A   D
But if you refuse Him and then comes the end,
                    A   E   A
There'll be no longer mercy but judgment, my friend.

COME AND SEE

1.
   A
The little woman at the well
        D   A
Thought her past life was hid,

But here sat a Savior
                          E
Who knew all the things she did.
A
As her life unfolded,
    D   A
The water jug set down,

She became a witness
   E   A
To everyone in town.

Chorus
   A
Come and see! Come and see!
        D   A
What great things He has done!

He calmed the waters;
           E
He stopped the sun.

  A
He opened blinded eyes.
  D   A
Yes, He's the One.

Come and see! Come and see!
                  E   A
What great things He has done!

2.
   A
The war clouds hanging o'er our world.
        D   A
Seems black to me and you.

But nothing is impossible;

There's nothing He can't do.
A
I can rest in Jesus,
      D   A
And the Spirit's fruits you'll see

As His love, joy, and peace
     E   A
Become alive in me.

3.
   A
If you don't know the peace
 D   A
That I sing about,

Then you don't know the reason
                 E
Why I sing and shout.

   A
The signs of time tell me
  D   A
He'll soon come again.

I've gotta be ready
     E   A
To leave this world of sin.

PRAISE THE LORD, I'M GOING UP HIGHER!

1.
  A
They say beyond Earth's atmosphere
             E
You need a shield from the heat.
                  A
The shield that I have can't be beat.
                            E
The Hebrew children tried it when thrown in the fire.
                   A
Praise the Lord, I'm going up higher!

Chorus
  A   E
Praise the Lord, I'm going up higher!
               A
Going up there and joining a heavenly choir.
  A7   D
I won't be here when the world's on fire.
  A   E   A
Praise the Lord, I'm going up higher!

2.
  A   E
God told Noah to build a boat,
             A
To pitch it in and out so it would float.

Carol J. Hill Chatman

                        E
Then came the floods on that great day,
                            A
And Noah just up and sailed away.

3.
A   E
I'm all ready and waiting to go,
                           A
Washed in His blood, made white as snow.
                          E
I'll meet you there on that great day,
        A   E   A
When all God's children are called away.

FEED MY SHEEP

1.
   G   C
The night's coming on; the day is gone.
  D   G
Now it's time to rest.
                       C
The ninety and nine are safe in the fold,
        D   G
But the shepherd says, "Where are the rest?"

Chorus
   G   C
Feed my sheep, feed my sheep.
   D   G
So many are hungry and cold.
          C
Feed my sheep, feed my sheep.
 D   G
Bring them all safe to the fold.

2.
   G   C
So many are bruised, tattered, and torn.
    D   G
Their path has been so rough.

Carol J. Hill Chatman

```
                        C
They'll never make it safe to the fold
     D          G
Unless we care enough.


3.
  G         C
Out on a hill, lonely and bare,
        D                   G
Is the little sheep who's gone astray.
                        C
Unless we search and find him soon,
     D          G
He'll never find his way.
```

LIVING WATERS

1.
  C
Men down through the ages
      F   C
Have always searched to find

Some secret to keep them young
      D   G
And give them peace of mind.
    C
But till they meet the Master
     F   C
And fall down at His feet,

They'll never find these waters
    G   C
So cool and sweet.

Chorus
  C
Living waters flowing
  F   C
From the throne of God.

Living waters
      D   G
Where other feet have trod.

Carol J. Hill Chatman

C
Our fathers dug these wells,
    F   C
And now it's plain to see,

There's living water flowing out
    G   C
For you and me.

2.
  C
I hear that Ponce De León
  F   C
Looked the whole world o'er

Searching for a fountain of youth.
    D   G
It brought him to our shore.
    C
He went away discouraged
    F   C
Because he couldn't find

This youth-renewing water
      G   C
That is yours and mine.

3.
  C
Springing wells of water
F   C
Isaac did find

As he unstopped the wells,
    D   G
His father left behind.

    C
The enemy began to fight,
  F   C
So he marched forth again.

And they found wells of water
    G   C
In barren, desert sand.

I CAN'T MAKE IT BY MYSELF

1.
   A
The load gets, oh, so heavy, Lord,
      E
And no one round to share
                        A
All the pent-up feelings in my heart.

But if I'll stop and listen,
     E
And give You half a chance,
                        A
You'll renew my strength as at the start.

Chorus
A
I can't make it by myself.
                            E
I'm sure You've known that all along.
D
But with You beside me,
   A
The Spirit to guide me,
E   A
I know today I can't go wrong.

2.
   A
Lord, it seems there are times
      E
When I cannot go on.
                    A
Then I remember what You said,

How the devil cannot steal
 E
One that is Your own,
                A
So I firmly take that step ahead.

3.
A
I can see the finish
      E
And my Jesus just ahead.
                A
Makes me glad I didn't dare to stray.

The race has now been worth it
    E
As I look upon His face,
                    A
And know that He has led me all the way.

I CHOOSE TO BE HAPPY

1.
```
   C              F         C
Worldly pleasures once had me blind;
                D       G
All the good things I'd left behind.
 C                        F        C
All I saw were bright lights, not eternity
 F          C         G         C
Till the Spirit of the Lord beckoned to me.
```

Chorus
```
C                    F           C
I choose to be happy; I choose to be free.
                D         G
I choose Jesus because He chose me.
C                         F       G
I choose to be free from sin; He set me free!
F    C         G             C
I just can't believe how He's changed me.
```

2.
```
C                   F         C
I was far from the fold, wandering astray,
                D       G
When the Master came my way.
```

```
C                         F              C
```
I was trapped in Satan's snare; my eyes were blind.
```
   F            C              G                C
```
Jesus took me in His arms and left my chains behind.

3.
```
C                     F        C
```
If Jesus comes today to call for me,
```
                           D       G
```
He'll find me watching, happy and free.
```
C                     F           C
```
If some cloudy day you find I'm gone,
```
   F            C              G              C
```
You'll find me with the saints there round the throne.

Carol J. Hill Chatman

THE BRIDE OF CHRIST

Chorus
  A
Son, go and get her,

And bring her back to us.
                            E
Please be as quick as you can.

The supper is ready,

And we are all waiting
                                 A
To welcome her home to this beautiful land.

1.
  A
Please swing the gates open,

And bring out the trumpets.
                        E
The supper is about to begin.

Since my Son is King,

King of all ages,
                               A
For seven long years we'll feast without end. So …

2.
A
The announcement's been made;

The Bride has been chosen,
                                      E
And she is adorned in pure white.

She's made herself ready.

The Groom now is coming.
                                      A
The celebration could begin before night! So …

CREATE WITHIN ME, LORD

1.
G   C
In the beginning, when God created,
G
Everything was good,
                 D
And everything was new.
  G   G7
Then Satan came,
    C
And he distorted.
    G   D   G
So Lord, I'm giving my heart back to You.

Chorus
    G   C
Create within me, Lord, a right spirit.
    G   D
Create within me, Lord, a new heart.
    G   C
Create within me, Lord, a right spirit.
    G   D   G
Create within me, Lord, a brand-new heart.

2.
```
G              C
Very soon now Jesus is coming
  G                         D
Back to this earth to make it anew.
  G           G
Satan will be gone.
          C
There'll be no more sinning.
  G
Lord, I want to live
          D         G
In that new land with You.
```

IF YOU'VE STRAYED

1.
   C
If you've strayed so far away,
           F
And you're thinking someday,
     C   G
I'll come back to the Master on my own,
     C
Just remember that He said.
        F
You don't know what is ahead,
       C   G   C
And you surely can't make it on your own.

Chorus
  C
Just remember in His Word,
      F
How He fed the little bird,
    C   G
And how the lilies, too, with color strown.
        C
Don't you know He loves you more,
      F
And He's knocking at your door
        G   C
And asking you just to come on home.

2.
  C
Satan's powers are much too strong,
          F
And He'll woo your heart along
    C   G
Until with mighty chains you'll find you're bound.
    C
Let Jesus in today.
        F
He will break those chains away
        C   G   C
And prepare for you a place on higher ground.

Carol J. Hill Chatman

GET YOUR HOUSE IN ORDER

1.
C
Now some people talk about going to the moon
     F   C
And someday inhabit Mars.

And they say before long
        D   G
We'll be shooting for the stars.
    C
And me—with my funny little grin—
    F   C
I just sit around and smile.

I know the trip I'm planning
    G   C
Will miss theirs by a mile.

Chorus
F
Get your house in order.
   C
One day we're going to fly.

While the world's in desperation,
                 G
His coming draweth nigh.

My God Can Deliver

  C
They don't know what they're talking about
            F
When they talk about you and I.
  C
Get your house in order.
      G   C
One day we're going to fly.

2.
  C
Now when God spoke to Noah,
   F   C
He said He'd seen the sin,

And that no one in the whole wide world
      D   G
Lived right outside of Him.
    C
The neighbors didn't believe him
    F   C
And wouldn't get in his boat;

But they were all knocking at his door
    G   C
When it began to float.

3.
  C
Our preachers all preach so hard;
        F   C
The world begins to rant and rail.

They say, "He's trying to tell us
     D   G
There's a literal, burning hell.

      C
Now we don't have to listen
    F   C
To all that scary tale."

But they'll be hiding in their caves
          G   C
When our ship begins to sail.

HALLELUJAH! HALLELUJAH! HALLELUJAH!

1.
```
C              F
John said he went to that city
          G              C
And was brought before the throne.
C              F
A voice saying, "Praise our God,"
       G
Made old John feel at home.
     C              F
When he heard that voice talking,
G          C
He could hardly wait.
              F
He'd already learned that song
       G          C
Outside that pearly gate.
```

Chorus
```
C         F        G        C
Hallelujah! Hallelujah! Hallelujah, Lord!
          F        G
Hallelujah! Hallelujah! Hallelujah! Then …
C         F        G        C
Hallelujah! Hallelujah! Hallelujah, Lord!
              F                G           C
With the angels round the throne, we'll sing it once again.
```

Carol J. Hill Chatman

2.
```
C              F
```
I remember back at home
```
        G            C
```
When Grandma used to pray.
```
   C            F
```
Now she's gone to be with Jesus;
```
G
```
I'll see her someday.
```
   C          F
```
When we gather over yonder,
```
     G            C
```
Round that shining throne,
```
                  F
```
And Grandma begins her singing,
```
   G          C
```
Then I'll feel at home.

3.
```
   C             F
```
Now I want to be one of that number.
```
G        C
```
I can hardly wait!
```
C              F
```
I'll be standing in the corner,
```
   G
```
Right next to the gate.
```
C          F
```
I will be the one that's singing
```
     G          C
```
Loudest in the crowd,
```
            F
```
So if you're trying to find me,
```
        G              C
```
You'll hear me singing out loud.

JOHN SAW A CITY

1.
G
John saw a city
          C   G
Coming down from God in the sky.
C   G
Six thousand miles round the walls, we're told,
                              D
That stand two hundred feet high.
 G
John saw a city;
 C   G
You and I living there.
          C   G
The throne of God, in the midst of it all,
           D   G
Will be heaven, I do declare.

Chorus
 G
I've already made preparations.
           C   G
My ticket's prepaid, I've been told.
         C   G
I've already been invited
                              D
To walk on those streets made of gold.

170   *Carol J. Hill Chatman*

```
G
All my friends can go with me.
      C              G
The price is no object, you see.
      C              G
It's already been paid on Golgotha's Hill,
          D          G
And for you and me it is free.


2.
  G
John saw a city,
      C          G
And what a sight to behold.
   C             G
God shall wipe all the tears from our eyes,
                      D
And we shall never grow old.
  G
John saw a city
        C             G
Where all things were made new.
          C          G
We're invited to drink at the fountain of life,
      D              G
In a home God's building for you.


3.
  G
John saw a city
          C              G
Where the Lamb of God is the light.
     C       G
No sin will ever enter its gates,
                     D
And there'll never come a night.
```

My God Can Deliver

```
  G
John saw a city.
     C              G
He saw it as it came into view.
    C          G
This is the city that Jesus talked about,
         D            G
He was going to build for you.
```

THERE IS NO EXCUSE

1.
   G
When you meet men on the street,

And you tell them about Jesus,
                       D
They'll give you reasons why
                       G
They are living in sin.

These will seem so small

When you stand before Him.
               D
They'll be the reasons why
                 G
You won't enter in.

Chorus
    G   C
There is no excuse
                  G
If you don't know the Savior.
      D
There is no excuse
                 G
If you won't let Him in.

        C
When on that judgment day,
        G
God sits before you.
        D
He'll say, "Depart from me."
        G
There is no excuse.

2.
G
Men are working so hard down here;

They are striving for riches.
        D
Contented with worldly gain,
        G
They're neglecting their souls.

But these things will all corrupt

And tarnish with using.
        D
So small, and yet enough,
        G
To keep them out of God's fold.

Carol J. Hill Chatman

OURS IS THE VICTORY

1.
G
I was once in bondage;

Satan had me bound.
  C
Then I met the Master;
         D
He turned my life around.
   G
Now I'm shouting happy
    C
As everywhere I go.
   D
My sins have all been washed away,
     C   G
And I want the world to know.

Chorus
  G
Ours is the victory,

Marching with the Lord.
  C
Walking in the Spirit,
        D
Leaning on His Word.

```
   G                C
With the full armor of God I stand.
   D
Over the next mountain,
    C           G
I see the Promised Land!
```

2.
```
G
If you are discouraged,

Let me tell you what to do.
   C
Call upon the Master,
                      D
And He will strengthen you.
G
Satan cannot stay
           C
Where Jesus is found.
   D
He'll have to flee when you
   C           G
Walk to higher ground.
```

Carol J. Hill Chatman

I JUST TALKED TO HEAVEN

1.
   D
When Israel was led out of bondage,
                     A
They cried for water and bread.
       D   G
When God sent both in abundance,
 D   A   D
They knew their God wasn't dead.

Chorus
 D
Well I just talked to heaven this morning,
                  A
And this one thing I know—
     D   G
My God is alive and well;
    D   A   D
His Spirit bears witness in my soul.

Well I just talked to heaven this morning,
                      A
And my call, it went through just fine.
   D   G
If you're having trouble, my brother,
 D   A   D
It's all on your end of the line.

2.
  D
Elijah, he called down the fire;
                              A
Daniel stopped the mouths of the lions.
            D   G
They picked up their receiver to heaven,
    D   A   D
And their God was right on the line.

3.
  D
Belshazzar said, "Bring out the vessels;
                       A
We're having a party so grand."
        D   G
The cups were anointed for service;
  D   A   D
They shook in Belshazzar's hand.

Carol J. Hill Chatman

THE KING IS COMING

1.
G
On a day so long ago,
                     C
As Jesus neared Jerusalem, we're told,
    G   D
The people began to shout, "Hosanna to the King!"
                       G
They brought Him a donkey that He might ride,
               C
And spread their coats on either side,
         G   D   G
And spread palm leaves to show honor to Him.

Chorus
  G   C   G
The King is coming to Jerusalem.
                         D
Open wide the gates; make room for Him.
      G
Can't you see the grand parade
    C
As all of heaven is arrayed,
 G   D   G
Marching back to earth to reign with Him?

2. (recitation)
    G   C
Well one day He's marching back out of heaven.
                G
Not to face the mockers and scoffers, nor to have
                                       D
His beard plucked by the very men He came to save,
                          G
Or turned away by His own people.
                    C
But He's coming back triumphant with glory and honor.
    G   D   G
Victorious to the very gates that were once closed to Him,
                C
Where they said, "Away with Him. Give us Barabbas."
    G
He's coming back to sit on the throne of David,

And He'll be welcomed as the
        D
King of Kings and the Lord of Lords
           G
Because that's who He really is.

(*Repeat Chorus*)

WHAT SHALL I GIVE TO HIM?

1.
   C   F   C
When I stand before Jesus at the foot of the cross—
                       G
My body so worn and bent—
    C   F   C
I'll stand there with nothing but a soul that is lost.
              G   C
What shall I give to Him?

Chorus
  F   C
What shall I bring to the Master?
               G
My heart's so full of sin.
  C   F   C
When I come and kneel at His feet,
       G   C
What can I give to Him?

2.
  C   F   C
The wise men came bringing their gifts
          G
Of gold and frankincense.

   C   F   C
When I face Him some sweet day,
             G   C
What shall I bring to Him?

3.
   C   F   C
A woman named Mary saw Him one day;
            G
She gave her all to Him.
   C   F   C
Her sins—which were many—she laid at His feet.
           G   C
That's what she gave to Him.

Carol J. Hill Chatman

HELP ME STAND IN THE GAP

1.
C
By the stripes that were laid on my Savior's back,
    F   C
I stand before you whole.

By the blood that He shed on Calvary,
                        G
He saved my poor lost soul.
     C
And now I am walking in the light;
   F
I give Him full control.
C
I'll stand strong, and by His help,
     G   C
Bring others to the fold.

Chorus
        F
Help me stand in the gap and make up the hedge
      C
When Satan comes around.
        F
Help me stand in the gap and make up the hedge
    C   G
When others can't be found.

   C
Those who win the victory
        F
Are the ones who stand their ground.
         C
Help me stand in the gap and make up the hedge
    G   C
To tramp that devil down.

(*Recitation*)
C   F
You know, sometimes we as God's people
        C
Think we've gone our limit.

We've given all we can give, prayed all we can pray,
       G
And the burden's not been lifted.
      C   F
But praise God! He said in His Word (2 Chronicles 20:17),
        C   G   C
"Ye shall not need to fight in this battle … Stand ye still
    G   C
And see the salvation of the Lord with you!"

(*Repeat Chorus*)

MY LORD IS COMING SOON

1.
    C   F
My eyes are fixed upon the Eastern sky;
    G   C
I know that His appearing draweth nigh.
                                      F
I'll soon be telling this old world goodbye
    G   F   G   C
And going to a city where I won't ever die.

Chorus
    C   F
My Lord is coming soon to take His bride away;
        G   C
My Lord is coming soon to bring a brighter day.
                                F
My Lord is coming soon to put an end to sin.
G
I want to live with you, Lord,
      F   G   C
Where my tomorrows never end.

2.
C   F
In God's Book my name is written down,
    G   C
And one day my feet will leave this ground.

              F
I'll be meeting Jesus way up in the sky.
     G   F   G   C
Oh say, are you ready to tell this world goodbye?

ISAIAH CHAPTER 9 TRUTHS

Chorus
   C   F   G   C
Wonderful, Counselor, Mighty God,
            F   G
Everlasting Father, Prince of Peace (Isaiah 9:6).
     F   C
Of the increase of His government there is no end,
   G   C
No end ever to His peace (Isaiah 9:7).

1.
   C   G   C
A child is born unto us;
       F   G
A son is given, and they say (Isaiah 9:6)
    F   C
Upon the throne of David, He will reign
   G   C
With judgment and with justice in that day (Isaiah 9:7).

2.
   C   G   C
The people who walked in the dark (*Spoken:* That's us!)
    F   G
Have seen a great light.

          F   C
They that dwelled in the land of the shadow of death;
   G   C
Upon them this light is shining bright (Isaiah 9:2).

STAND YE STILL

1.
```
G                      C
If you're struggling in a battle,
    D                  G
And it seems all hope is gone,
                              C
Just stand firm, and wait for God to conquer.
            D                G
He's never late; the battle has been won.
```

Chorus
```
   G                          C
Stand ye still, and see the Lord's salvation
       D                 G
That He will show to you today.

You need not fight.
                    C
Fear not for He is with you
       D                  G
And goes before you all the way.
```

2.
```
G                        C
If the Creator of this great universe
    D                G
Could create just even me,
```

My God Can Deliver

                C
Then surely He can fight my battles
      D   G
And bring me forth victoriously.

3. (*Recitation*)
  G
You know, one time David was commanded
                    C
To get over behind the mulberry bushes and just wait.
     D
And God said that when he heard the sound of "a going"
             G
In the tops of those bushes to march forth, and He'd go
               C
Before him into battle (2 Samuel 5:24). David won
              D   G-C-G
That battle for God Himself fought for him.

(*Repeat Chorus*)

MY RACE IS ALMOST RUN

1.
  C   F   C
Time has come for me to lay my armor down,
        F   C
To pick up my robe and receive my crown.
                 F
'Cause I'm walking in His sight,
C   F
No more battles will I fight.
 C   F   C
And my race is almost run,
          F   C
And my race is almost run.

Chorus
C   F   C
It will be joy in the morning.
       F   G
It will be joy 'cause I know
 C   F   C
Jesus is coming for His children.
      F   C
And I'm ready to go,
      F   C
And I'm ready to go.

2.
```
  C         F            C
Though the hills are steep that I have to climb,
         F            C
And the way seems rough as it upward winds,
           F
I know He's by my side—
  C          F
No reason to fear or hide.
  C          F    C
And my race is almost run,
              F    C
And my race is almost run.
```

Carol J. Hill Chatman

MOTHER'S ECHO

1.
   C
A mother, she lay dying
        G
As the children gathered round.

They could hear her whisper,
                   C
Though she hardly made a sound.
              F
She told them of heaven,

Of her home awaiting there.
               C
As she was crossing over,
  G   C
They heard her declare,

Chorus
C
I want to see Jesus,
    G
The One who died for me.

To walk in His presence
             C
Through all eternity.

I want to see heaven,
      F
See the streets made of gold.
C   F
I want to walk, I want to talk
    G   C
While the endless ages roll.

2.
  C
The room, it was so silent
   G
As the mother's voice ceased.

A smile that settled on her face
      C
Spoke to them of peace.

It made them think of angels' wings
      F
As they took mother home.
     C
And the echo of her words
   G   C
Came to them from the throne.

MOTHER'S BURDEN

Chorus
    C   F
Could this be that mother of yours, boy,
        G   C
Who's wasting your life out in sin?
                       F
Could this be that mother of yours, girl,
        G   C
Who's pleading, "God, please bring them in"?

1.
   C   F
There was a lovely young maiden.
     G   C
She bore the cross in her life.
                      F
Now her family is scattered and broken,
       G   C
And she's torn by trouble and strife.

2.
   C   F
She's always been faithful to you, Lord.
    G   C
She planted the seed of Your Word.

                                      F
Then she watered it with her own tears, Lord,
    G   C
So all of her family have heard.

3.
 C   F
Lord, You see the load that she carries.
        G   C
She's carried that burden too long.
                                F
Please take that load from her shoulders,
        G   C
And replace it, Lord, with a song.

Carol J. Hill Chatman

SOMETHING WRONG IN AMERICA

1.
   A   E   A
They can't read the Bible in our classrooms,
        E   A
Yet our judges make decisions every day
        D   A
That give freedom to smut and pornography,
    B   E
And to kill: "You have a right to choose," they say.

Chorus
        A   E   A
There's something wrong in America.
                    D   E
There's a plague that's spreading o'er our land.
     D
Let's get down upon our knees
  A
And cry, "Oh, God, please
                E   A
Send revival once again to fallen man."

2.
   A   E   A
Our children are out stealing and killing;
E   A
No one home to teach them how to pray.

```
     D                     A
Moms and dads are just too busy;
  B                           E
After all, there's all these bills to pay.
```

```
3.
A           E           A
If the men who formed our constitution
          E             A
Could return and tell us why it read,
         D             A
"One nation under God, indivisible,"
              B                        E
They would say, "It was because we knew God led."
```

OLD GOSPEL SHIP

1.
A   E   A
Elijah knew the time was fast approaching.
        E   A
He said, "Elisha, stay right here and wait for me.
        D   A
For the Lord, He hath sent me to old Jordan;
       E   A
A chariot in the sky waits for me."

Chorus
A   D   A
Oh, the old ship of Zion soon is coming.
 E   A
This is going to be her final trip.
   D   A
Oh, tell me, are you ready for her leaving?
               E   A
Have you booked passage on this old gospel ship?

2.
A   E   A
Enoch was a man who walked with God;
   E   A
His steps took him higher every day.

```
       D                         A
The Bible says he was not for God took him.
                    E           A
The gospel ship had just passed his way.
```

3.
```
A                E            A
Jesus said when we see these signs approaching,
            E              A
Then we'll know the time is drawing nigh.
          D                  A
The old gospel ship will soon be sailing.
                  E         A
Keep your eye upon the Eastern sky.
```

94. PRAISE

1.
F   C
The trumpeters and singers were as one
         F
In praising and thanking the Lord.

They lifted up their voices

With the trumpet and cymbals

And instruments of music,
 C   F
And praised God, saying:

Chorus
 F   C
For He is good! For His mercy endureth forever
            F
For He is good! For His mercy endureth forever.
           B♭
For He is good! For His mercy endureth forever,
    F   C   F
And the glory of the Lord filled the house.

2.
  F   C
The priest could not minister by reason of the cloud,
                                  F
For the glory of the Lord filled the house.

The Levites—which were singers—arrayed in white linen,

All with their cymbals, psalteries, and harps.

And a hundred twenty priests,

Sounding out with trumpets.

(Can you imagine?)
 C   F
All praised God, saying:

THE TRUTH ABOUT HELL

1.
  C   F
Hell holds no beauty,
     G   C
No happiness, no peace.
            F
Hell captures hopelessness
     G   C
In a night of fright—no cease.

No water there to cool the tongue.
   F
No hope of sweet release.
      C
This is hell.
  G   C
This is hell.

2.
  C   F
Hell holds her victims
     G   C
In chains of despair.
        F
Hell has no escape
      G   C
For those who enter there.

You'll never see a baby's smile
        F
In this nightmare with no end.
        C
This is hell.
  G   C
This is hell.

3.
  C   F
Hell has no music,
    G   C
No happy songs to sing.
              F
Hell is continual burning
    G   C
That never, never ends.

No parties in that atmosphere
       F
That's filled with Satan's clan.
     C
This is hell.
  G   C
This is hell.

MY FOUNDATION

1.
   G   C   G
When the waves around me beat,
 C   G   D
I hear my Savior's voice so sweet,
   G   C   G
Saying to fear not, for He's by my side.
 C   G   D   G
He'll calm the raging, swelling tide.

Chorus
G C
I fear not
 D   G
For I stand
C   G
On a foundation
 D   G
Not made by man.

2
   G   C   G
When my eyes behold the night,
  C   G   D
Faith is my lamp, shining so bright.

```
    G              C      G
Fears all vanish when I look, I see
  C      G      D      G
Jesus my Savior standing by me.
```

Second Chorus
```
G C
I fear not
 D    G
For I stand
  C      G
On a foundation
 D       G
Not made by man.
C G
Amen!
```

HE'S SO WONDERFUL

1.
C   G
Everything He created He said was good.
                                    C
Everything fit perfectly, just like it should.

And He gave it all to me,
                F
Showing His love so wonderfully.
    C   G   C
My God, He is so wonderful!

Chorus
C
He's so wonderful!
                             G
He made the earth; He made the seas.

He's so wonderful!
                            C
He made the flowers; He made the trees.

He's so wonderful!
                           F
He made the birds; He made the bees.
    C   G   C
And then, God—He made me!

2.
```
   C                      G
I sold myself in bondage to sin.
                                C
Jesus went to the cross to set me free again.

He bought me back at Calvary,
           F
Broke the chains that bound me.
     C    G       C
My God, He is so wonderful!
```


3.
```
   C                    G
I was just a little lump of clay
                             C
Till God took the time to mold me that day.

He breathed the breath of life in me,
            F
Made me what He'd have me be.
     C    G       C
My God, He is so wonderful!
```

Carol J. Hill Chatman

MY RETIREMENT HOME

1.
G
I've heard about my mansion that's being
  C   G
Built for me on high.
      C   G
I've heard about the landscape
                  D
Of my home up in the sky.
G
I know the decorator;
      C   G
He's the best in all the land.
    C   G
And when it comes to mixing colors,
    D   G
The rainbow's in His hand.

Chorus
G
I'm going to a place up there
    C   G
Beyond the starry skies.
    C   G
I'm going to a place up there
                D
Where storm clouds never rise.

   G
I'm going to a land where there will
C   G
Never come a night.
   C   G
Won't you come and go with me?
       D   G
I'm about to take my flight.

2.
    G
If you're looking for vacation spas,
    C   G
My home is in the town
   C   G
Where all the elite—heaven's best—
          D
Are always hanging round.
   G
There'll be no thieves, no honky-tonks,
     C   G
No booze, no drugs, you see.
    C   G
For everything that will defile,
   D   G
He has cleaned out for me.

THE KEY TO MY HEART

1.
  C   F
When I gave to Jesus the key to my heart,
  C   G-G7
He gave His keys to me.
     C
He gave me the keys
   F
To open all of heaven's best—
  C   G   C
All for my one bent key.

Chorus
  C   F   C
When I gave to Jesus the key to my heart,
F   G-G7
He just came inside of me.
    C
He picked up all the brokenness
      F
And mended all the hurts inside
     C   G   C
And made it all new for me.

2.
C
I'd held so tightly to that key.
      F
Satan tricked me so many times;
 C   G-G7
He'd made a fool out of me.
     C
He broke my heart in pieces,
       F
Trying hard to destroy my life.
     C   G   C
But, I gave Jesus that key.

3.
  C
I now can open heaven's best,
    F
And all of its blessedness,
       C   G-G7
Since Jesus gave me His keys.
    C
He gave His very life to buy
    F
The things that now can satisfy,
C   G   C
All for my one bent key.

Carol J. Hill Chatman

GOD IS WATCHING OVER ME

Chorus
  F
God is watching over me
    C
To hear me when I pray.
  F
God is watching over me
    G
To lead me all the way.
C
Every time I've needed Him,
     F   C
He knows the way I take.
  F   C
God is watching over me
     G   C
To guide the steps I make.

1.
C
In this day of trouble,
        F   C
When the enemy abounds,

I've found that my faith in God
      D   G
Is the greatest thing around.

     C
Whenever the way looks dark,
  F   C
I go to Him in prayer.
      F   C
And always when I've needed Him,
      G   C
I've found Him waiting there.

2.
     C
The snares of the enemy
  F   C
Abound on every hand.

He knows he doesn't have long to work
   D   G
In this old, troubled land.
  C
He's trying to snare my feet
  F   C
And lead me far astray.
    F   C
But someone guides my footsteps
      G   C
That I'm making every day.

HE'S MY REFUGE

Chorus
  A
He's my refuge in the midst of trouble.
        D   A
He's my shelter in the midst of the storm.

He's my Rock, my sword, my shield;
        D   A
He's my wheel in the middle of the wheel.
      E   A
He's the arm that I lean on.

I.
  A
When the way is oh, so lonely,
       D   A
And the mountains I can't climb,
       D   A
When my steps are oh so feeble,
       B   E
And I've reached a steep incline.
    A
Then I rest upon His shoulders,
    D   A
And I feel Him lifting me,

     D   A
Now I have no fear or worry
         E   A
'Cause I know He stands by me.

2.
A
Jesus said to His disciples
       D   A
Just before He went away,
               D   A
That the road they traveled would not be easy
       B   E
As they walked from day to day.
        A
He said to remember He'd not leave them.
          D   A
And when it seemed their strength was gone
        D   A
Just to lean closer upon His promise,
      E   A
And He'd help them to go on.

Carol J. Hill Chatman

BABY JESUS IN A MANGER

1.
C
Baby Jesus in a manger
                         F
Was clothed with flesh like man.
      G
The star that shone upon him there
                         C
Would light the way for man.

The angels heralded His coming.
                            F
The shepherds marked His birth.
  G
Wise men came from afar
                    C
To greet the King of earth.

2.
  C
Mary was His mother.
                    F
Joseph stood there, too—

Astounded by this miracle
                      C
That God said He would do.

This was not just any babe
                         F
Who lay there on the hay.
  G
This was God's greatest gift
                          C
That He gave that Christmas day.

3.
   C
From the palace to a stable
                   F
Jesus came that day.
  G
From the splendors of heaven
                    C
To a manger full of hay.

What would ever cause a king
                        F
To step down from his throne?
  G
It had to be the greatest love
                    C
This world has ever known.

I WANT TO BE WITH YOU, LORD

1.
    A
When this old world is shaking
          E
And the rocks and mountains fall;

I'll be hiding in Jesus,
             A
He's the shelter from it all.

When men are shaking with fear
            D
And have no place to hide;
      A
I'll be sitting at the supper
        E   A
Where the Lamb will take His bride.

Chorus
D
I want to be with you, Lord,
      A
Where no storm clouds ever rise.
D
Sitting at the Master's feet
         E
Up yonder in the skies.

   D
Feasting at the table
     A
Prepared by God on high.
     E
Meeting all our loved ones
              A
At that reunion in the skies.

2.
A
If you're building on the sand,
 E
Jesus taught one day;

When the storms begin to come
              A
You'll surely be swept away.
      G
You'll seek shelter in the rocks,
              D
But in that day you can't hide.
         A
The only place of safety
  E   A
Is at the Savior's side.

ONLY IN YOUR NAME, LORD

   G   C
Only in Your name, Lord,
               G
Only in Your name, Lord.
          D
Only in Your name, Lord,
         G
Only in Your name.
          C
Devils fear and tremble,
            G
Mountains melt before me
       D
Only in Your name, Lord,
        G
Only in Your name.

WHAT THE ENEMY MEANS FOR BAD

   D
What the enemy means for bad
              G   D
We claim for good to those who love the Lord.

What the enemy means for bad
                    E   G
We claim for good; we're standing on God's Word.
      D
When the devil comes in like a roaring lion,
 G
God wins the battle every time.
     D
What the devil means for bad
              A   G
We claim for good to those who love the Lord.

Carol J. Hill Chatman

TOPICAL INDEX

Admonition

Get Your House in Order	165
Get Ready, Children	21
If You're Living Just for Things	67
If You've Strayed	163
Oh, Be Careful, Little Children	48
Old Gospel Ship	199
Too Late	143

Anticipation

Count Me In	105
I'll Be Looking for Him in the Morning	135
I'm Going Home	17
I Want to be With You, Lord	219
In a Million Years	50
Include Me	62
It Won't Be Long Now	59
My Race Is Almost Run	191
Praise the Lord, I'm Going Up Higher!	148
We Are Predestined	44

Adoration

Hallelujah! Hallelujah! Hallelujah!	168
I Love Just to Sit	57
Praise	201

Atonement

Come Carry My Cross	76
Living Waters	152
Whatever the Cost	7

Children's Songs

He's So Wonderful	207
I've Got the Attributes of God	120

Christmas

It Was Just a Little Baby	5
Baby Jesus in a Manger	217

Cleansing

Stains	125

Compassion (of Jesus)

He's Alpha and Omega	127
Jesus's Tears	19

Decisions

Decisions That We Make	34
I Choose to Be Happy	157
There Is No Excuse	173

Dedication

What Shall I Give to Him	181
Your Presence	13

Deliverance

No God Can Deliver	1
The Burden's Been Lifted	115

Easter

He's No Longer in the Manger	97
Who Will Roll the Stone Away?	36

Ever-Present Help

A Present Help	71
God Is Watching Over Me	213
He's My Keeper	46
He's My Refuge	215
Jesus On My Side	141
Let Him Walk Upon Your Waters	52
My Foundation	205

Evolution

My Thoughts on Evolution	94

God's Love

God, You So Loved	55
It's Written Down	11
The Gift of Choice	118
Why Heaven Cared Enough	9

God's Majesty

Stand Ye Still	189
The Lord Reigneth	80

Grace

Help, I Need Grace	108
I Will Never Walk Alone	38

Guidance

I Can't Make It By Myself	155
Lord, Guide My Footsteps	84
Lord, We're Your Children	30

Heaven

I've Read in My Bible	40
John Saw a City	170
My Retirement Home	209

Hell

The Truth About Hell	203

Intercession

Something Wrong in America	197

Invitation

Come and See	145
How Many Times?	73
Jesus, Jesus	82
Jesus Is Calling	86
What Will Your Answer Be?	139

Jesus's Power

Only in Your Name, Lord	221
You Can	113

Jesus's Provision

There Is Room	65

Jesus's Return

He Walks the Mountaintops	100
My Lord Is Coming Soon	185
The Bride of Christ	159
The King Is Coming	179

Love for God

I Love You	32

Mothers

A Counter of Minutes	129
Mother's Burden	195
Mother's Day Song	28
Mother's Echo	193

Prayer

Chris's Letter to God	131
Dear Lord	92
Fire on the Altar	42
I Just Talked to Heaven	177
Jesus, I've Sat on Your Doorstep	90
Problem Solver	133

Prophecy

Isaiah Chapter 9 Truths	187

Redidication

Create Within Me, Lord	161
Love	88
Take the Pieces, Lord	15

Rejoicing

I've Got That Old-Time Religion in My Soul	137

Restoration

I Feel Restoration Coming On	103

Salvation

Keeper of the Door	69
The Blood Has Been Applied	23
The Key to My Heart	211

Sin

Trash Can	78

Trials

Tried and Tested	25

Valor

The Battle Is the Lord's	111
Help Me Stand in the Gap	183
Mighty Man	122
Put on the Armor	3

Victory

Ours Is the Victory	175
We Have Power O'er the Enemy	58
What the Enemy Means for Bad	222

Witness

Feed My Sheep	150
I've Got That Old-Time Religion in My Soul	137

INDEX

A

A Counter of Minutes	129
A Present Help	71

B

Baby Jesus in a Manger	217

C

Chris's Letter to God	131
Come and See	145
Come Carry My Cross	76
Count Me In	105
Create Within Me, Lord	161

D

Dear Lord	92
Decisions That We Make	34

F

Feed My Sheep	150
Fire on the Altar	42

G

Get Ready, Children	21
Get Your House in Order	165
God Is Watching Over Me	213
God, You So Loved	55

H

Hallelujah! Hallelujah! Hallelujah!	168
He Walks the Mountaintops	100
He's Alpha and Omega	127
He's My Keeper	46
He's My Refuge	215
He's No Longer in the Manger	97
He's So Wonderful	207
Help, I Need Grace	108
Help Me Stand in the Gap	183
How Many Times?	73

I

I Can't Make It By Myself	155
I Choose to Be Happy	157
I Feel Restoration Coming On	103
I Just Talked to Heaven	177
I Love Just to Sit	57
I LoveYou	32
I Will Never Walk Alone	38
If You're Living Just for Things	67
If You've Strayed	163
I'll Be Looking for Him in the Morning	135
I'm Going Home	17
In a Million Years	50
Include Me	62
Isaiah Chapter 9 Truths	187
It Was Just a Little Baby	5
It Won't Be Long Now	59

It's Written Down — 11
I've Got That Old-Time Religion in My Soul — 137
I've Got the Attributes of God — 120
I've Read in My Bible — 40
I Want to be With You, Lord — 219

J

Jesus, Jesus — 82
Jesus Is Calling — 86
Jesus, I've Sat on Your Doorstep — 90
Jesus On My Side — 141
Jesus's Tears — 19
John Saw a City — 170

K

Keeper of the Door — 69

L

Let Him Walk Upon Your Waters — 52
Living Waters — 152
Lord, Guide My Footsteps — 84
Lord, We're Your Children — 30
Love — 88

M

Mighty Man — 122
Mother's Burden — 195
Mother's Day Song — 28
Mother's Echo — 193
My Foundation — 205
My Lord Is Coming Soon — 185
My Race Is Almost Run — 191
My Retirement Home — 209
My Thoughts on Evolution — 94

N

No God Can Deliver — 1

O

Oh Be Careful, Little Children — 48
Old Gospel Ship — 199
Only in Your Name, Lord — 221
Ours Is the Victory — 175

P

Praise — 201
Praise the Lord, I'm Going Up Higher! — 148
Problem Solver — 133
Put on the Armor — 3

S

Something Wrong in America — 197
Stains — 125
Stand Ye Still — 189

T

Take the Pieces, Lord — 15
The Battle Is the Lord's — 111
The Blood Has Been Applied — 23
The Bride of Christ — 159
The Burden's Been Lifted — 115
The Gift of Choice — 118
The Key to My Heart — 211
The King Is Coming — 179
The Lord Reigneth — 80
The Truth About Hell — 203
There Is No Excuse — 173
There Is Room — 65
Too Late — 143
Trash Can — 78
Tried and Tested — 25

W

We Are Predestined — 44
We Have Power O'er the Enemy — 58
What the Enemy Means for Bad — 222

What Shall I Give to Him	181
What Will Your Answer Be?	139
Whatever the Cost	7
Who Will Roll the Stone Away?	36
Why Heaven Cared Enough	9

Y

You Can	113
Your Presence	13

CPSIA information can be obtained
at www.ICGtesting.com
Printed in the USA
FSHW021154180122
87733FS